Cats in Cross Stitch

Cats in Cross Stitch

Sally Harman

Michael O'Mara Books
in association with the RSPCA

This book is dedicated to all cats but in particular to
Penny, Smudge, Hobbes, Cleo, Ali, Lucky, Softy,
Misty, Ellie, Juliet, Krystal, Maya, Archie, (last but
never least) Elle, and all their respective
owners, especially Tiffany.

First published in Great Britain in 1997 by
Michael O'Mara Books Limited
9 Lion Yard
Tremadoc Road
London SW4 7NQ

A CIP catalogue record for this book is available from the British Library.

ISBN 1-85479-619-4

1 3 5 7 9 10 8 6 4 2

Designed and Typeset by Clive Dorman & Co.
Photographs by Helen Pask

Printed and bound in Hong Kong by Paramount Printing Group Limited

Contents

Foreword

I was very pleased to be asked to write a foreword for this book. Cats have always been favourites of mine. They strike me as being very well organized – they love their creature comforts, warmth, luxurious surroundings and, of course, good food. If these are supplied in adequate quantities the owner is rewarded with a loving faithful friend.

Our own cat, Penny, a tortoiseshell, had a bad start in life by being abandoned in a flat in a back street in London. Thankfully the neighbours heard her cries and called the RSPCA who had to break in to rescue her. Penny was in a pitiful state and for a while we were not sure if she would live. She spent a couple of weeks in the hospital before being adopted by my wife who fell in love with her. Once she came home she never looked back. Being a typical tortoiseshell she has a mind of her own and is boss in our house. She still shows some signs of insecurity and needs a cuddle if her routine is upset. Cats in general are lovely animals to treat when they are ill as they respond so well to tender loving care and nursing.

Although I have a tortoiseshell my favourite cats are ginger. They are so handsome to look at and nearly always have a very friendly temperament. We had a ginger tom in the hospital recently that had fallen over seventy feet and broken both front legs. Within less than a week of the operation to repair them he was up on his feet and greeting everybody who came near with the loudest purr you have ever heard. We were unable to find his owners, but it was a joy to see him re-homed with a family with a garden. The last I heard of him he was fully recovered and climbing trees with glee. Fortunately, as he has grown older he has learned to exercise caution and can negotiate his way down safely.

I am sure that those who buy this book will have many hours of enjoyment. Cats are beautiful creatures and the designs in these pages fully do them justice.

David Grant

Introduction

Cats are truly magnificent creatures and this book is a celebration of their beauty, charm and intelligence, as well as their fortitude in the face of adversity. The cats featured have all come into contact with the Royal Society for the Prevention of Cruelty to Animals (RSPCA) in various parts of Britain and for a number of different reasons.

The *Getting Started* section provides clear information regarding various fabrics, threads, stitches and techniques used in cross stitch. In addition, professional tips have been included, where appropriate, in order to give the reader a better understanding of certain aspects of cross stitch. It is intended that this will help the readers who may wish to produce a design based on their own cat, having first tried some of the charted projects.

As well as making the designs accessible to the beginner, the author has taken care to present work which will appeal at all needlework skill levels. Innovative ideas have also been included in the book. For example, ideas for a Cafetière Cover, a Clock, a Photograph Album and a Christmas Stocking are included alongside more familiar applications of cross stitch work. As well as providing a coloured chart and full instructions for each project, the author has added a footnote with alternative suggestions for working the design. On page 68, one of the alternative suggestions has been stitched and is illustrated alongside the original version, which featured in *All About Cats* magazine. The alternative is worked in cross stitch using wool and large-holed tapestry canvas so that, with the addition of a simple checkered border, the 4 x 6 in picture becomes a 14 in square cushion.

The final part of the book provides full instructions for creating a professional finish to the stitched pieces. Readers who usually pass items for framing on to others, or only make the occasional greetings card, will not be daunted by the information given in this section. It is intended that they will be stimulated into expanding the range of their work by using pre-purchased glass paperweights, box lids, clock mechanisms, and by covering books. This book can therefore provide a stepping-stone to adopting a more adventurous and creative approach to cross stitch work.

Getting Started

Cross stitch continues to increase in popularity so many readers of this book will be new to the craft. *Getting Started* will therefore be a useful guide for the beginner, but the more experienced stitcher may also find the information below helpful.

FABRICS

It is possible to work cross stitch on a wide variety of fabrics as well as paper, plastic and netting. However, this book concentrates on the more familiar ones which are readily available in needlework shops and via mail order suppliers.

Aida

The easiest fabric to use is Aida, an evenweave fabric with clearly defined stitch holes, designed both for ease of work and counting of stitches or spaces. Its regular nature ensures that all your stitches will be evenly sized and thus the design will not be distorted. It comes in a variety of 'count' sizes. The 'count' number refers to the number of stitches per inch it provides. Therefore, the larger the 'count', the smaller the stitch. Aida is also available in a wide range of colours and in a new non-fraying format, Aida Plus.

Linen

The comment made about 'count' sizes needs further clarification when considering Linen 'counts'. For example, a 28-count Linen can be used as a direct substitute for a 14-count Aida since conventionally cross stitch on Linen is worked over a pair of the Linen threads, making 14 stitches to the inch. The advantage of Linen, as well as its undoubted high quality appearance, is that it provides flexibility so that some greater detail may be achieved in parts of a design by working the stitches over single threads rather than over pairs of threads. It also allows a very small piece of work to be stitched with a considerable amount of detail, as in the case of the Desk Tidy. However, Linen is more difficult to use than Aida because the fabric's threads move easily, increasing the chance of distortion, and more care needs to be taken when carrying threads across the back of your work because of Linen's more transparent nature.

Tapestry (Needlepoint) Canvas

Like the other fabrics, this comes in various 'count' sizes, usually referred to as holes per inch (hpi). Mono canvas has a single thread between each hole; double thread has two (usually interlocked), to reduce canvas thread movement. The canvas used for the black-and-white cat Cushion is double thread. The larger holes are used for stitching, not the smaller holes created by canvas threads overlapping.

THREADS

In the same way that various fabrics can be used for cross stitch, a wide variety of threads can also be used – everything from the finest silk to ribbon, raffia or string. The threads you will find in this book are the more conventional ones and again are readily available from good needlework shops and suppliers.

DMC Stranded Embroidery Thread

This is a most useful embroidery cotton, loosely twisted thread with six strands and having a high-lustre finish. It is best used in lengths no longer than 18 in (45 cm) and for the designs in this book it is divided and used as either 1, 2 or 3 strands. After cutting the required length, the two best ways to divide up the six strands are as follows:

(i) Grasp the middle of the yarn's length and gently pull away, one at a time, the number of threads required; or

(ii) Hold one end of the length of yarn very firmly with one hand and with the other find the tip of an individual strand. Holding the other strands tightly, pull the strand through your gripping fingers.

Having extracted your required threads, put the set of ends together in preparation for threading.

DMC Crewel Embroidery Wool

This is a beautiful soft yarn of fine wool which is extremely useful for any piece of cross stitch which is likely to have considerable handling or dusting when made up into a finished item. Again, use lengths no longer than 18 in (45 cm).

DMC Flower Thread

This is a non-mercerized cotton with a matt finish. It comes in a wide range of colours and one strand of it is roughly equivalent to two strands of stranded cotton.

DMC Tapestry Wool

This is a suitable yarn for a cross stitch Cushion (although it is more usually used for half-cross stitch). Use lengths of 18 in (45 cm) or less.

DMC Metallic Thread

This can be used as the equivalent of a single strand of stranded embroidery thread but it can also be used in double, triple or, with difficulty, quadruple lengths. Alternatively, for very fine work, it can be untwisted and divided into its component three strands. In this book, however, it is used straight from the reel and two lengths of it are stitched together.

EQUIPMENT

For very small pieces of work the minimum of equipment is required. For small projects worked on Aida the use of an embroidery hoop is a matter of personal choice. For larger pieces of work a hoop is recommended, but by no means is it compulsory if you feel it hampers your working and you can stitch neatly without one. However, continual direct handling of fabric not only increases the chance of your work getting dirty but it also breaks down the structure of the fabric's dressing, which is there to retain the relative stiffness, and thereby the shape, of the fabric.

Embroidery Hoops

These are made in various sizes and the smaller ones are easier to handle. If working a larger piece, however, it is better to use an appropriately larger frame. The size of the fabric you are working on will be a guide to the most appropriate hoop to use. In order to fit a hoop, a piece of fabric must be larger (or longer in one direction) than the hoop's diameter.

If you have a design which you think is likely to be in an embroidery hoop for a long time, cover the fabric with a similar-sized piece of either paper or thin cotton (Muslin is very good for this purpose) and then fit the fabric and its covering into the hoop together. Carefully expose the area to be stitched by tearing or cutting the protective paper or Muslin. This serves two purposes. It minimizes the damage done by the hoop and it keeps the unstitched area of the fabric clean, avoiding the need to wash it after stitching. Paper is obviously more readily available than Muslin but the noise made by rustling paper when handling your hoop can be distracting!

Rectangular Frames

If your fabric is too big for an embroidery hoop then you may want to use a rectangular frame. The rotating frames are useful for this purpose and plastic quilting frames are also worth considering. Alternatively, an old picture frame can be put into service. (If it is a very old frame, bind it round with masking tape to protect your fabric.)

Needles

Tapestry needles are blunt so that they do not split the thread of either the fabric or stitches already worked. The needles come in different sizes and you can purchase them in either a single packet with a range of sizes or packets containing needles of one size only. I find it useful to have several needles so that, if I do not use all of a length of thread in one area of stitching, that needle can be put to one side awaiting the need for that colour again. This avoids unthreading and re-threading yarn.

Thimble

I personally cannot work using a thimble and as a tapestry needle is blunt it is not essential to use a thimble for cross stitch. However, if you are used to working with one then continue to do so.

Air-soluble Pens

These are wonderfully useful for a variety of purposes. For example, you can use one to draw lines across and down the centre of a piece of fabric prior to stitching to make it easier to locate the centre and avoid the need for basting stitches which would later have to be removed. The pens usually give a purple line which will fade after a short period of time if your fabric has a large amount of dressing in its finish. Other fabrics, such as Linen, will often hold the coloured lines for several days – so be warned if you want to complete a gift in a hurry!

It is most important that you do not confuse this type of pen with embroidery marker pens (which often also give a purple line) as these are permanent or semi-permanent.

Translucent Graph Paper

This is available in a variety of sizes to correspond with cross stitch fabric and tapestry canvas 'counts'. You can use it to produce your own chart by placing it over a photograph or picture you wish to stitch. It will 'square-up' the image and you will find it useful if you wish to substitute other cats' faces in the clock design.

Scissors

A pair of small embroidery scissors with pointed blades is vital for the clean cutting of thread and also comes in handy for unpicking any stitches worked in error. A larger pair of sharp scissors is helpful for cutting fabric.

TECHNIQUES

Preparing your Fabric

Cut your fabric to the required size. After cutting the fabric I have always found it beneficial to remove any fold creases prior to stitching or placing the fabric in an embroidery hoop. You will usually have to iron a piece after stitching, but some of the fold creases can prove to be extremely obstinate and I prefer to tackle them with a wet cloth and a medium-hot iron without any stitches being present.

Mark the centre of your fabric by either drawing lines with an air-soluble pen or stitching lines of basting stitch. These lines should be midway along each edge and go to the midpoint of the opposite edge. Where they cross is the middle of your fabric. The midpoint of the chart can be found by following the line down from the midpoint arrows marked on the chart. Mount your fabric on a hoop or frame if using one.

Organizing your Threads

Having prepared your fabric you may find it helpful to organize your threads on a yarn holder. One way to do this is to count up the number of colours to be used and cut a piece of thin card to a suitable length. Allow ½ in (1 cm) for each colour plus an inch (2.5 cm) at the top and bottom. The piece of card should be approximately 2 in (5 cm) wide (see diagram below).

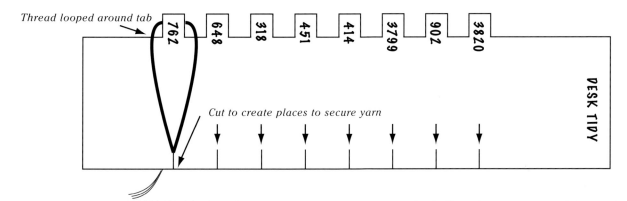

Thread looped around tab

762 648 318 451 414 3799 902 3820

Cut to create places to secure yarn

DESK TIDY

To make the yarn holder, cut one long side of the card to give the pattern shown above. On the opposite long side, cut ½ in (1 cm) into the card opposite the midpoint of each protruding 'tab'. You can write the number of the yarn in pencil on the tab (pencil allows you to re-use the same card for another project). Keep the colours in the order they appear on the chart key so that you can find them easily. Cut a length of each yarn shade, fold each one in half in turn and loop the doubled length around the tab, securing the ends by slotting them through the slit opposite. You can also write the title of the project on the end of the card so that if you are stitching more than one piece of work at a time, you do not confuse the yarns required. This allows you to keep the bulk of the skeins in a neat and clean condition.

Using a Chart

The charts in this book are given in colour, but because they are worked on different-sized fabrics it is important to remember that *the size of the chart is not necessarily the size of the finished design.* Unless otherwise stated, each coloured square represents one stitch, worked over one square of Aida or two threads of Linen. Lines of back-stitch are marked in narrow lines and half-cross stitch is indicated by a half-coloured square.

Having found the centre points of your fabric and charts, you are ready to begin to work the design. Some books recommend that you count up from the centre of your fabric and the chart, so that you work the design from the top downwards. This minimizes the handling and any contact with stitches already made, but I find it a slightly boring method and prefer to work from the centre outwards so that I am free to work in any direction I desire from the centre point. The main advantage of working from the centre is that you can be sure of getting the correct position on the fabric for your work. (You can always work from the midway horizon downwards and then turn your work upside down to complete the other half.) Whichever way you prefer to work, you will probably find it helpful to stitch any White areas last.

THE STITCHES

Beginning and Ending Threads

Diagrams are given on the facing page for cross stitch, back-stitch and French knots, but before stitching you will need to know how to begin and end your threads. To start stitching, tie a knot in one end of your thread. Insert the needle down into the front of the fabric 1 in (2.5 cm) away from where you are making your first stitch and in the direction you will be working. *The knot should be on the front of your work.* Bring the needle up into the first stitch hole and then work your first stitches towards the knot. When you have completed five or six stitches, look at the back of your work to check that the yarn between the knot and your first stitch is held secure by the backs of the stitches. If it is, turn your work over again and hold the knot firmly, away from the fabric. Remove it by cutting the thread with sharp scissors. If it is not secure, continue stitching until it is. To finish off a thread, take it to the reverse side of your work and carefully thread it through the back of nearby stitches.

Cross Stitch

(NB: Ensure that all your top diagonals are worked in the same direction.) Make each stitch one by one (A), rather than working with a series of half-crosses and then doubling back to make full crosses(B). (This ensures that the cross 'sits' well in the square of the fabric and reduces the chance of distorting the fabric.)

Bring the needle up at 1, down at 2, up at 3 and down at 4.

Try to maintain an even tension in your work. If it is too loose it will look untidy and if it is too tight your fabric may pucker and end up being distorted in shape.

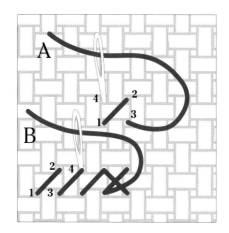

Back-stitch

Bring the needle up at 1, down at 2, up at 3 and continue as required.

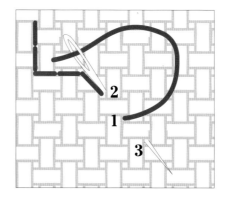

French Knots

Bring the needle up where you wish to make the knot. Hold the thread taut in your left hand, needle in your right (or *vice versa* if left handed). Place the needle behind the taut thread, twisting the needle round the thread twice. Push the needle back down into the fabric very close to where it came up and, keeping the thread taut, take the needle to the reverse side of your work, *slowly*.

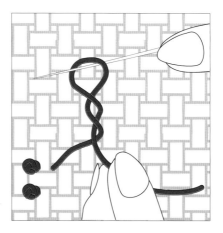

Picture Frames and Mounts

If you are a cat owner or cat lover you will no doubt have accumulated several cat pictures and greetings cards featuring them. Why not stitch these simple-to-make Mounts and Picture Frames so you can display some of your favourites rather than have them tucked away in a drawer? Alternatively, they make a suitable gift for a cat-loving friend. You can personalize the first Picture Mount by adding the cat's name and the year the photograph was taken.

14

MATERIALS

Paw Print Picture Mount, 8 x 6⅛ in (20.5 x 15.5 cm)

Sheet of Aida Plus in White or Ivory
DMC Stranded Embroidery Thread in 3042 Pale Purple or suitable alternative to match something in the photograph
Suitable picture frame
Masking tape

Mice Picture Mount, 5⅛ in (13 cm) square

Sheet of Aida Plus in White or Ivory
DMC Stranded Embroidery Thread in 613 Stone plus 2 appropriate shades to match the photograph (334 Blue and 436 Ginger were used for the mount illustrated)
Suitable picture frame
Masking Tape

Rectangular Picture Frame, 6⅛ x 8¼ in (15.5 x 21 cm)

Sheet of Aida Plus in Light Grey
DMC Stranded Embroidery Thread as Follows:

> 472 Lime Green
> 3820 Gold
> 3827 Pale Ginger
> 3776 Ginger
> 666 Red
> 646 Dark Grey
> 648 Grey

Double-sided adhesive tape
Mountboard, cut to the required size of the finished frame

Square Picture Frame, 6⅛ in (15.5 cm) square

Sheet of Aida Plus in Red
DMC Stranded Embroidery Thread as for Rectangular Picture Frame but substituting 793 Blue for 666 Red
Double-sided adhesive tape
Mountboard, cut to the required size for the finished frame

You will also need a DMC tapestry needle, size 24, for any of the above.

WORKING THE CROSS STITCH

Prepare the sheet of Aida Plus by marking out the area needed to display the photograph. The best way to do this is to measure your photograph and then create a paper template which measures ½ in (1.25 cm) less in each of the two dimensions. Place this template in the centre of the Aida Plus and mark the corner positions of the paper with two large stitches in each corner. (You can use an air-soluble pen if you prefer.) DO NOT CUT THE AIDA PLUS AT THIS STAGE. Begin working the chart, working round the frame or mount.

Use two strands for the Picture Mounts.

Use three strands for the Picture Frames except for the 3820 Gold which is worked using a single strand.

Below: Key for Rectangular Picture Frame

𝓚ey
DMC numbers underlined indicates back-stitch

 472   3827   666   648

 3820   3776   646

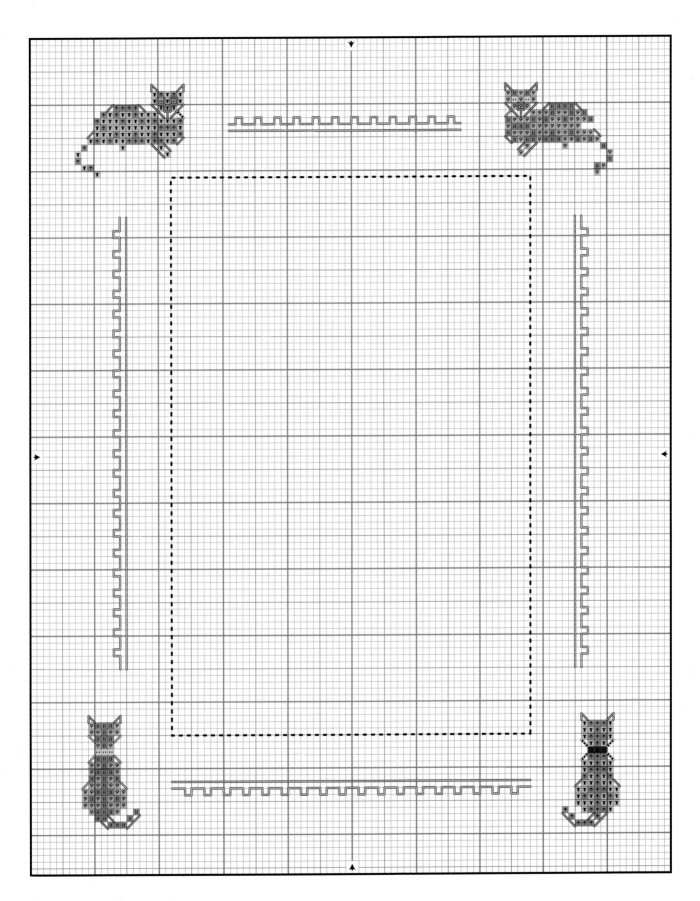

Rectangular Picture Frame

FINISHING THE WORK

Picture Mounts:

Using a pair of small-bladed sharp scissors, carefully cut out the central area, cutting along the lines of the Aida Plus, from corner mark to corner mark. Place the photograph in position and attach to the back of the Aida Plus using masking tape. Trim the outer edges of the Aida Plus if required. Place the mount and photograph in the frame.

Picture Frames:

Using a pair of small-bladed sharp scissors, carefully cut out the central area, cutting along the lines of the Aida Plus. Trim the outer edges of the Aida, to adjust the size and/or straighten the edges. Trim your mountboard, if necessary, so that it is the same size as the Aida Plus. Attach strips of double-sided adhesive tape to the reverse side of the Aida Plus, but to side edges and bottom only. When positioning the strips, place them ⅜ in (1cm) away from the central area to allow space to slide in the photograph. Remove the protective strips and carefully place the Aida Plus on the mountboard. If a stand-up frame is desired, attach a further piece of board to the back of the mountboard, scoring it lightly where it is to bend. For a wall-hung frame, attach ring fixings to the back of the mountboard and thread with picture cord or wire. Slide the photograph into position and display or hang the finished work.

ALTERNATIVE SUGGESTIONS FOR THE DESIGN

The individual motifs can be used in a variety of combinations to decorate a number of small items, for example, the Aida strip on specially manufactured baby's bibs or a small mirror using Aida Plus.

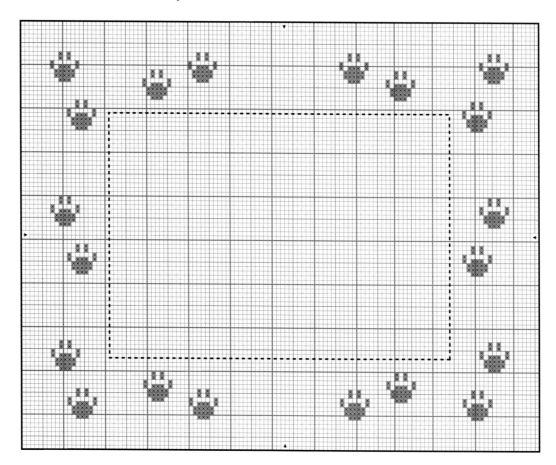

*Paw Print
Picture Mat*

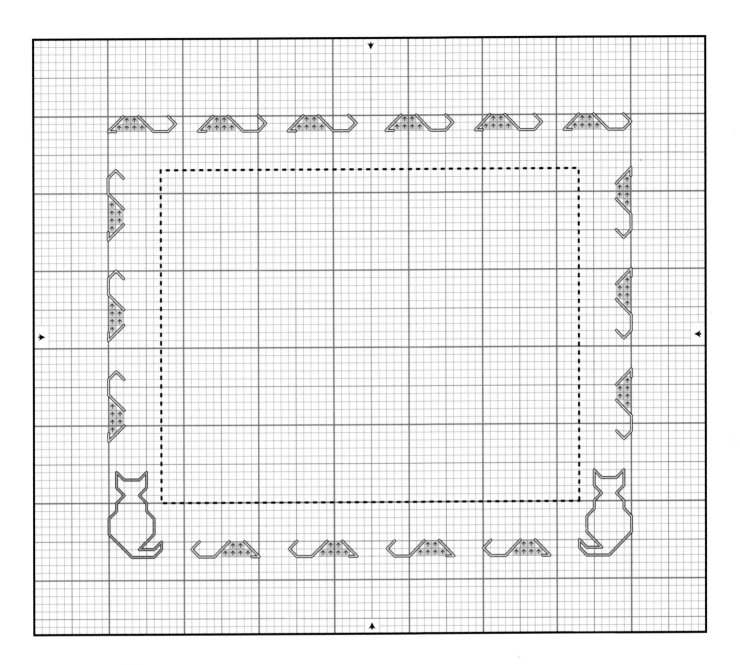

Mice Picture Mount

Christmas Sock and Stocking

Some cats think every day should be Christmas. You can make this festive time more special by making these present-holders. The sock will hold a new catnip toy, ping-pong ball and small bag of treats. The stocking is for the more demanding cat who expects to be indulged with a little extra!

MATERIALS

Sock, stitched area 4⅜ x 1⅝ in (11 x 4 cm)

Piece of Zweigart Decorative Band 2 in (5 cm) wide in Green, measuring 11 in (27.5 cm) in length

DMC Stranded Embroidery Thread as Follows:

310	Black
BLANC	White
3820	Gold
606	Red
553	Purple
807	Blue
964	Turquoise

Sock fabric of your choice and matching sewing thread

DMC Tapestry needles, size 24

Photocopy of the sock template enlarged by 400% onto thin card

Stocking, stitched area 5¼ x 1½ in (13.5 x 4 cm)

Piece of Zweigart Decorative Band 2¼ in (5.75 cm) wide in Red, measuring 13 in (33 cm) in length

DMC Stranded Embroidery Thread as follows:

353	Pink
BLANC	White
807	Blue
989	Green
904	Dark Green
3031	Brown
841	Dark Mushroom
543	Flesh

Stocking fabric of your choice and matching sewing thread

DMC Tapestry needles, size 24

Photocopy of the stocking template enlarged by 400% onto thin card

WORKING THE CROSS STITCH

Following the chart, commencing ½ in (1.25 cm) away from the right-hand end of the strip, with the far right edge of the design.

Use two strands throughout.

FINISHING THE WORK

Cut out two pieces of either sock or stocking fabric, using the appropriate enlarged template (see diagram below). Make up the sock/stocking, right sides together, using a ½ in (1.25 cm) seam allowance. Trim the curved edges and turn rightside out. Turn the hem allowance over at the top edge so that the raw edge comes over the front of the sock/stocking. Press the hem allowance and seam. Attach the hanging ribbon to the hem allowance at the opposite corner to the toe. Sew the two ends of the band together using a ½ in (1.25 cm) seam and checking that it fits the sock/stocking top edge. Slip stitch to the sock/stocking top, covering the hem allowance at the top edge.

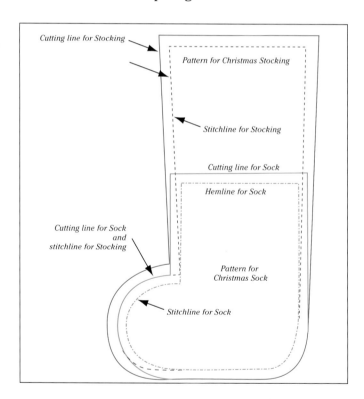

ALTERNATIVE SUGGESTION FOR THE DESIGN

Both these designs can be adapted to create Christmas greetings cards.

Opposite top: Christmas Sock
Opposite bottom: Christmas Stocking

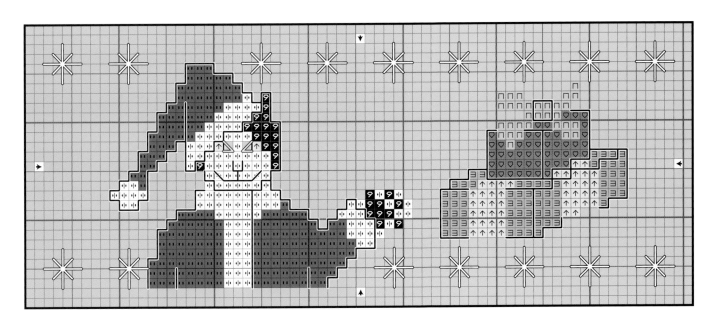

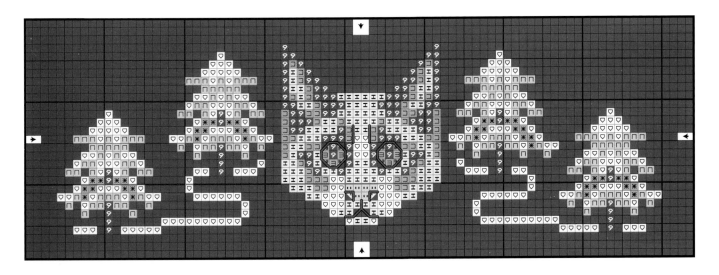

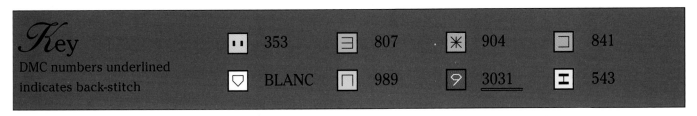

Greetings Cards

Cats are very patient creatures and fascinated
by water; these two characteristics have been
combined in the following design. These two
versions of the same design can be used either
as a general Greetings Card, a Get Well card or
a Good Luck greeting. If you are feeling
adventurous, you can vary the colours
of the bucket, flowers or cat to suit
your taste.

MATERIALS

*For design, stitched area 2⅝ x 3½ in
(6.5 x 9 cm)*

Piece of Zweigart 18-count Aida in Cream (for the White cat) or White (for the Black cat), 8 x 10 in (20.5 x 25.5 cm)

DMC Stranded Embroidery Thread as follows:

Black Cat

310	Black
3609	Pale Violet
893	Dark Pink
340	Mauve
3013	Pale Green
320	Dark Green
350	Red
746	Cream
840	Donkey Brown
613	Dark Mushroom
3045	Golden Brown
3821	Gold
3046	Pale Gold

White Cat

BLANC	White
727	Lemon
973	Yellow
742	Orange
471	Pale Green
3347	Green
996	Turquoise
921	Terra Cotta
407	Dusky Pink
840	Donkey Brown
613	Mushroom
3046	Pale Gold
371	Green Gold

DMC Tapestry needles, size 24
DMC Card blank in Dark Green or Cream
Double-sided adhesive tape for fixing

WORKING THE CROSS STITCH

Follow the chart, beginning in the centre of the Aida and working outwards. If stitching the White cat version, stitch the cat last.

Use two strands throughout but add back-stitch using one strand of 840 for the outer edge of the White cat.

FINISHING THE WORK

See *Finishing Your Work* section at the end of the book for details of fixing your stitched work to the card.

ALTERNATIVE SUGGESTION FOR THE DESIGN

These cats can also be used to decorate the oval in the Address Book.

Key DMC numbers underlined indicates back-stitch

	White Cat	Black Cat		White Cat	Black Cat
♀	BLANC	310	⅃	921	746
▪▪	727	3609	Ξ	407	840
▽	973	893	↑	840	613
⊒	742	340	V	613	3045
⊓	471	3013	△	3046	3821
✳	3347	320	◪	371	3046
▪◦▪	996	350			

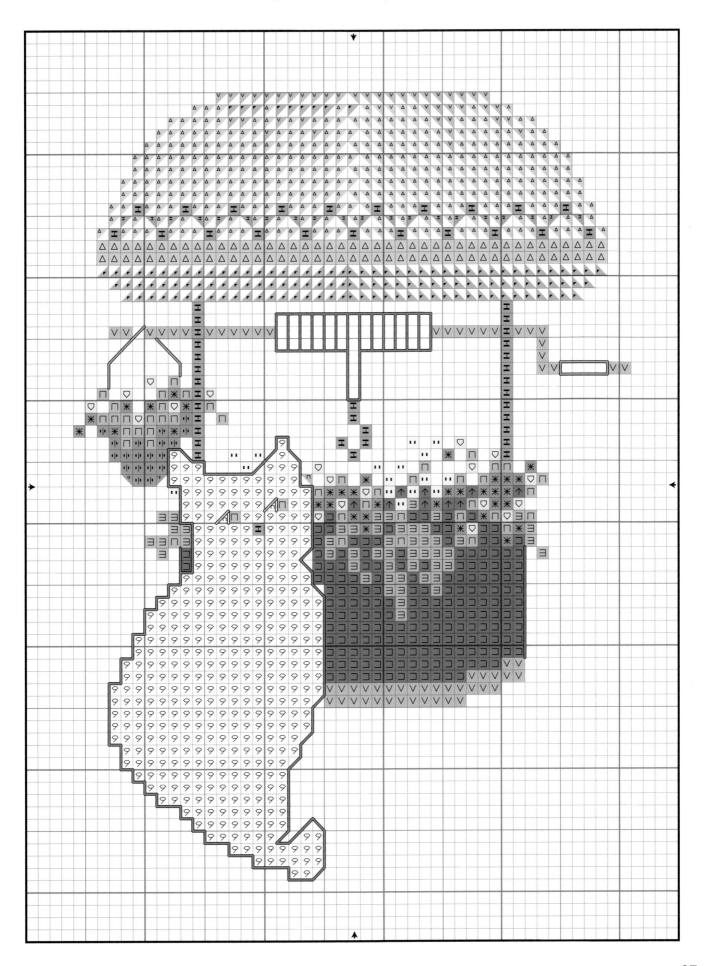

Calendar

This cat is intended to represent all cats who have contented lives after being rescued by the RSPCA. A calendar by its very nature is around for a year so this design has been worked in Crewel Embroidery Wool which will cope with regular dusting. As with the Greetings Cards in the previous project, there is no reason why you cannot change the colours to suit your own decor.

MATERIALS

For design, stitched area 3⅝ in (9 cm) square

Piece of Zweigart 14-count Aida in Emerald
Green, 9 x 11 in (23 x 28 cm)

DMC Crewel Embroidery Wool as follows:

8720	Royal Blue
8995	Kingfisher Blue
8997	Pale Blue
8419	Green
8327	Yellow

DMC Tapestry needles, size 20
Calendar blank
Picture Frame, inner measurement 4½ x 6½ in
(11.5 x 16.5 cm)

WORKING THE CROSS STITCH

Follow the chart, beginning with the first
horizontal row of the check background
which should be stitched 2½ in (6.5 cm) from
the top edge of the fabric. Continue to work
the cat and then complete the rest of the
background.

*Use one thread of Crewel Embroidery Wool
throughout.*

FINISHING THE WORK

See *Finishing Your Work* section at the end of
the book for details of preparing your work
for framing and other framing information.

ALTERNATIVE SUGGESTIONS
FOR THE DESIGN

The design itself is square and so it can be
used to make a pin-cushion or a pot-pourri
hanging for a room or wardrobe.

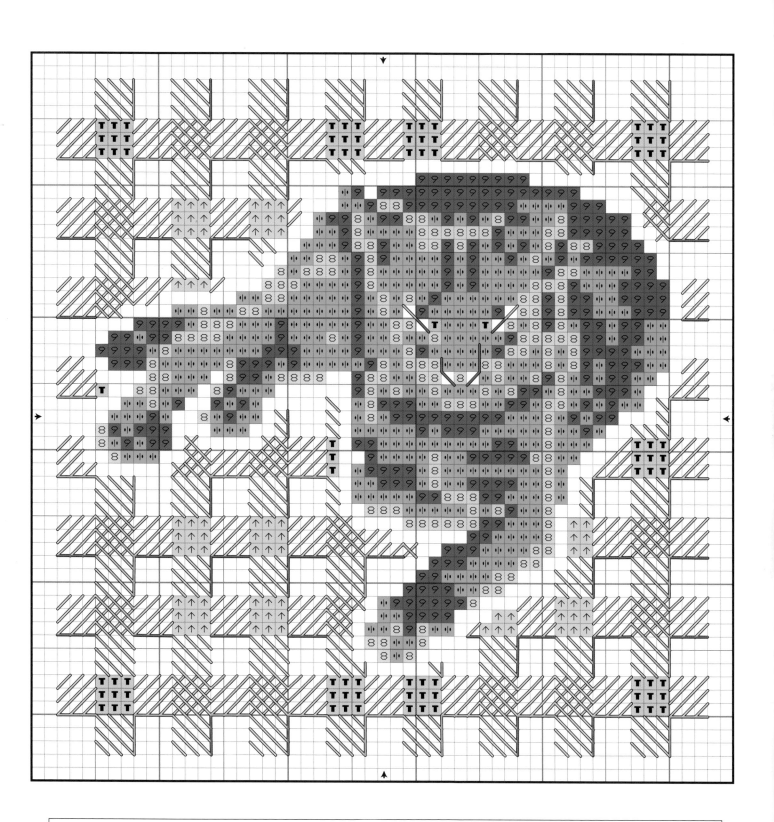

Key

DMC numbers underlined
indicates back-stitch

9	8720
8	8997
T	8327
•|•	8995
↑	8419

Address Book

Some kittens are so sweet and this one is just adorable! Her colours are such that she is an obvious choice to complement this Address Book or birthday book cover. An ideal present for any cat enthusiast.

MATERIALS

*For design, stitched area 2⅛ x 3¾ in
(5.5 x 9.5 cm)*

Piece of Zweigart 14-count Aida in Cream,
9 x 11 in (23 x 28 cm)

DMC Stranded Embroidery Thread as follows:

931	Blue
841	Dusky Pink
644	Palest Grey
3023	Pale Grey
647	Medium Grey
645	Dark Grey
535	Charcoal Grey

DMC Tapestry needles, size 24
Framecraft Address/Birthday Book blank

WORKING THE CROSS STITCH

Follow the chart, beginning in the centre of
the Aida and working outwards.

Use two strands throughout.

FINISHING THE WORK

See *Finishing Your Work* section at the end of
the book for instructions on covering a book.

ALTERNATIVE SUGGESTIONS FOR THE DESIGN

This design can be framed to make a
delightful small picture or sent as a greetings
card using an oval card blank.

𝒦ey

DMC numbers
underlined
indicates
back-stitch

| ▪▪ 931 | ‖ 644 | •|• 647 | ▪ 535 |
| ▽ 841 | ꟼ 3023 | ↑ 645 | |

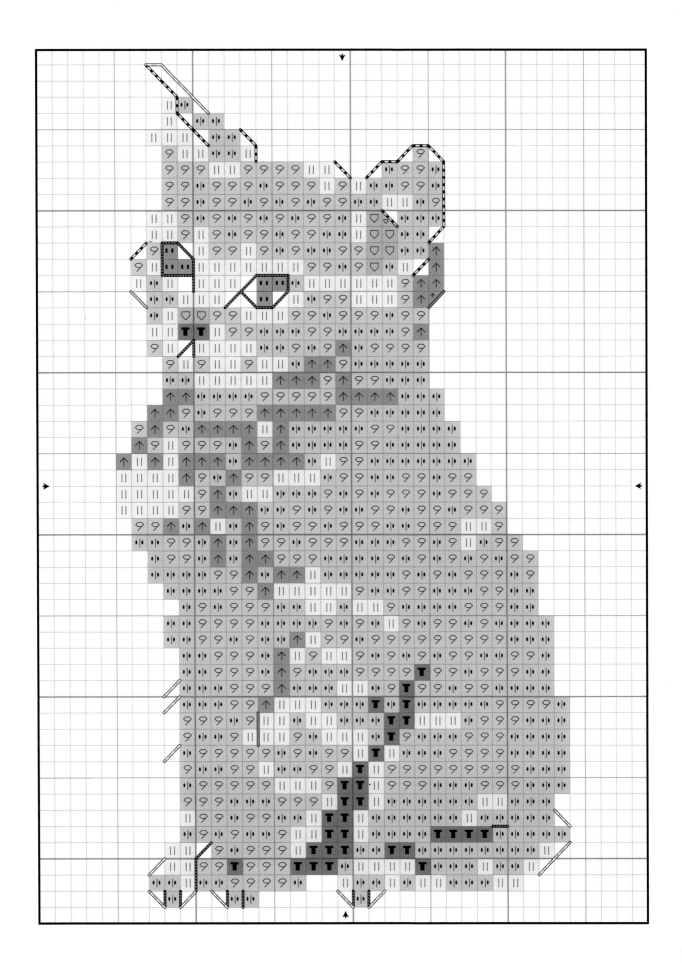

Paperweight

A paperweight makes an ideal gift and
this charming tortoiseshell cat surrounded by
poppies makes a decorative addition to
anyone's desk. Alternatively, it can simply
be used as an ornament.

MATERIALS

For design, stitched area 2⅝ in (6.5 cm) diameter

Piece of Zweigart 18-count Aida in Cream, 8 in (20.5 cm) square

DMC Stranded Embroidery Thread as follows:

310	Black
3371	Brown Black
3021	Dark Brown
840	Donkey Brown
613	Mushroom
3033	Palest Mushroom
822	Palest Stone
3828	Tobacco
422	Pale Tobacco
608	Orange
606	Scarlet
666	Red
3802	Purple
906	Green
472	Pale Green
758	Blush

DMC Gold Metallic Embroidery Thread (744)
DMC Tapestry needles, size 24
DMC Paperweight blank 3½ in (9 cm) diameter

WORKING THE CROSS STITCH

Follow the chart, beginning in the centre of the Aida and working outwards. Work the back-stitch round the eyes *after* completing the other eye colours.

Use two strands throughout.

FINISHING THE WORK

See *Finishing Your Work* section at the end of the book for instructions on fitting circular paperweight.

ALTERNATIVE SUGGESTIONS FOR THE DESIGN

This design can also be framed with a circular mount and a square frame to make a lovely picture. Alternatively, a geometric border can be added to make a pot-pourri holder or pin-cushion.

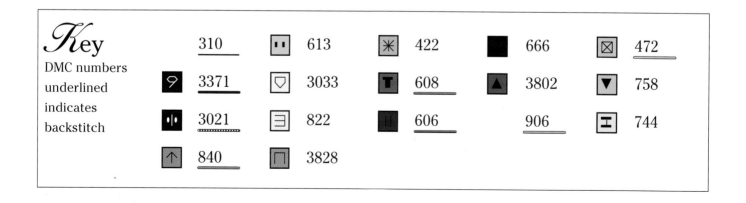

Key

DMC numbers underlined indicates backstitch

310	·· 613	✳ 422	■ 666	⊠ 472
9 3371	▽ 3033	T 608	▲ 3802	▼ 758
◖◗ 3021	目 822	606	906	工 744
↑ 840	⊓ 3828			

38

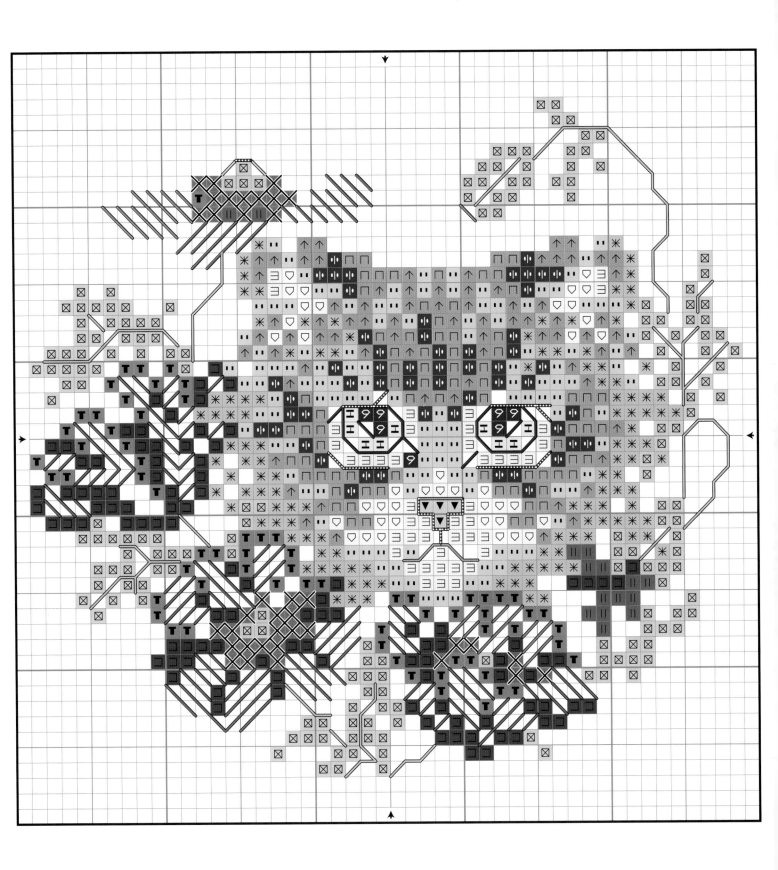

Candlescreen

*H*ere is a cat, doing what cats do best,
sleeping in a comfortable spot. This screen
makes a lovely decorative feature for the home.
It can be used as a backdrop for a hall table
decoration, preferably one using candles, or as
a decoration on a corner shelf or dresser.

MATERIALS

For design, stitched area 3 x 4½ in (7.5 x 11.5 cm)

Piece of Zweigart 14-count Aida in Rustico (shade 54), 9 x 11 in (23 x 28 cm)

DMC Stranded Embroidery Thread as follows:

677	Buttermilk
746	Cream
613	Pale Mushroom
422	Gold
434	Light Brown
921	Ginger
315	Dusky Plum
3803	Purple
3768	Blue
904	Dark Green
988	Light Green
523	Pale Sage

DMC Tapestry needles, size 24
Framecraft Candlescreen, Model WS Screen

WORKING THE CROSS STITCH

Follow the chart, beginning in the centre of the Aida and working outwards.

Use two strands throughout.

FINISHING THE WORK

See *Finishing Your Work* section at the end of the book for details of preparing your work for framing and other framing information.

ALTERNATIVE SUGGESTION FOR THE DESIGN

This picture will also fit inside the framed area of the Mirror.

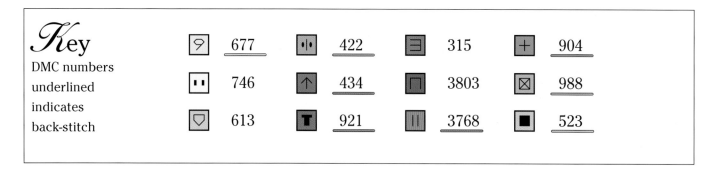

Key
DMC numbers underlined indicates back-stitch

⚲	677	⦙∙⦙	422	⊒	315	+	904
⁌∙∙⁍	746	↑	434	⊓	3803	⊠	988
▽	613	T	921	‖	3768	■	523

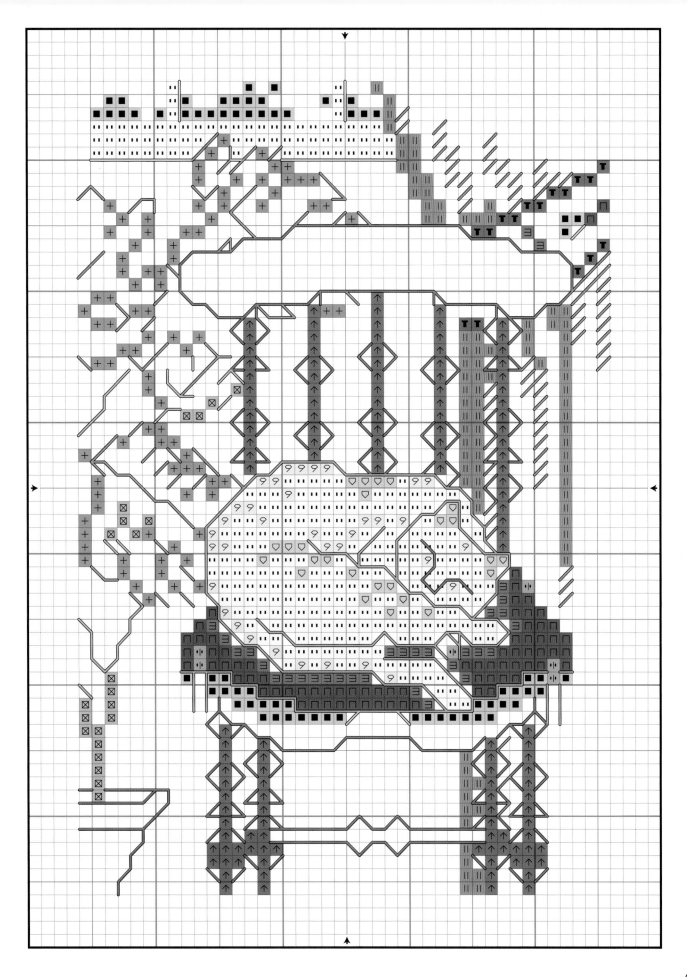

Wooden Needles & Scissors Box

Are you always misplacing your scissors
and needles? If so, this box with two thin flat
magnets hidden inside to secure its contents is
the answer to your problem. This half-Persian
cat decorating the inset is also used for the
Photograph Album Cover. So, if you are looking
for a pair of items as a gift for someone,
why not stitch both these projects?

MATERIALS

For design, stitched area 3 x 1⅜ in
  (7.5 x 3.5 cm)

Piece of Zweigart 18-count Aida in Cream,
  8 x 6 in (20.5 x 15.5 cm)

DMC Stranded Embroidery Thread as follows:

BLANC White
677   Buttermilk
676   Pale Ginger
436   Ginger
434   Dark Ginger
407   Dusky Pink
3821   Gold

DMC Tapestry needles, size 24
Framecraft Wooden Needles and Scissors
  Case, Model NSC
Double-sided adhesive tape for fixing

WORKING THE CROSS STITCH

Follow the chart, beginning in the centre of
the Aida and working outwards.

Use two strands for the cat's body, but the back-stitch outlining the cat should be worked using one strand.

FINISHING THE WORK

See *Finishing Your Work* section at the end of
the book for details of attaching your finished
piece to the box.

ALTERNATIVE SUGGESTION FOR THE DESIGN

Stitched on 14-count Aida to enlarge the
design, this would fit, horizontally, into an
oval card blank as used for the Greetings
Cards.

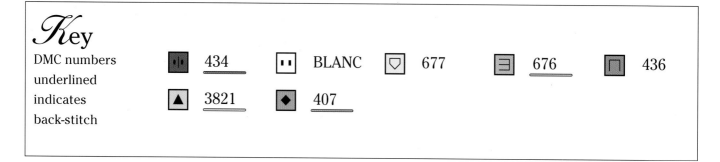

Key

DMC numbers
underlined
indicates
back-stitch

434   BLANC   677   676   436

3821   407

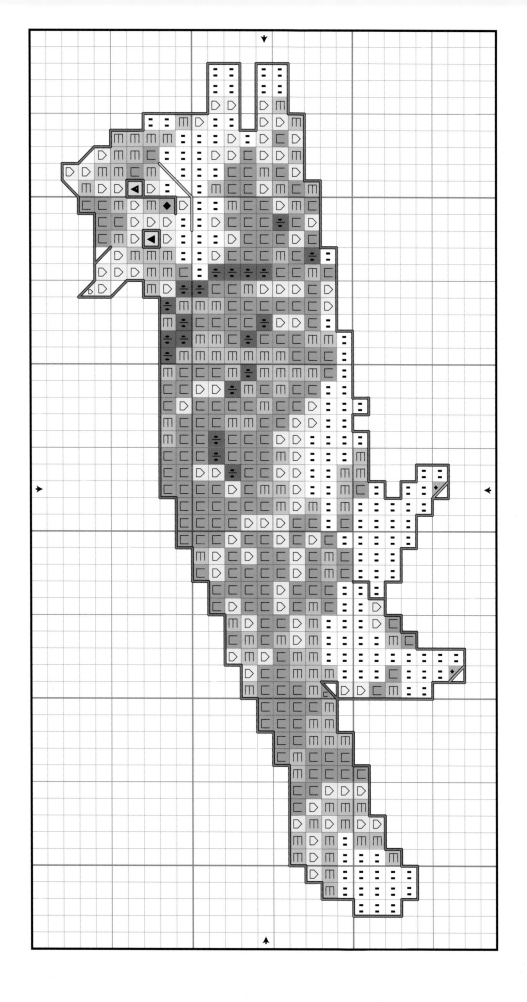

Silver-plated Box

Siamese cats always appear to have an air of superiority about them so it seems appropriate to use one for this box. The bargello-style background of muted shades is easy to work, but if preferred this can be omitted to give a simple elegant portrait.

MATERIALS

For design, stitched area 3½ in (9 cm) square

Piece of Zweigart 28-count Linen in Cream,
  9 in (23 cm) square

DMC Stranded Embroidery Thread as follows:

The Cat

799	Blue
ECRU	Ecru
3033	Pale Mushroom
841	Dark Mushroom
840	Donkey Brown
839	Medium Brown
838	Dark Brown
3371	Brown Black

The Background

3712	Rose Pink
761	Pale Pink
3823	Cream
676	Gold
320	Green
503	Turquoise Green

DMC Tapestry needles, size 24
Framecraft Silver-plated box, Model SF4

WORKING THE CROSS STITCH

Follow the chart, beginning in the centre of
the Linen and working outwards.

*Use two strands for the cat but work the
bargello-style background using one strand of
each of the colours.*

FINISHING THE WORK

See *Finishing Your Work* section at the end of
the book.

ALTERNATIVE SUGGESTIONS
FOR THE DESIGN

This design will fit the Teapot Stand. You can
stitch it as given in the chart, in which case it
will have an unstitched border between the
design edge and the Teapot Stand.
Alternatively, you can extend the bargello-
style background to fill the additional space.

  With some modification to the background
it can also be used for the Paperweight.

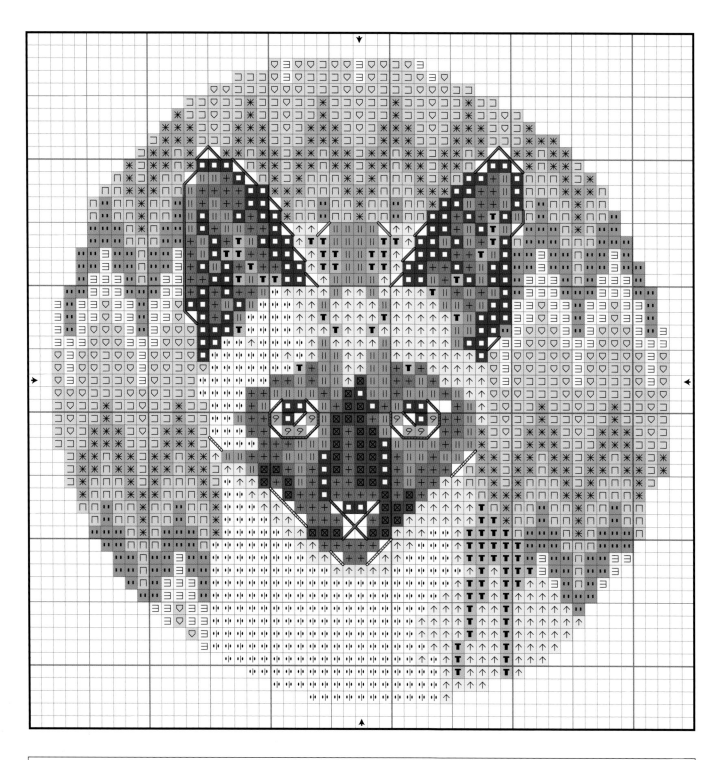

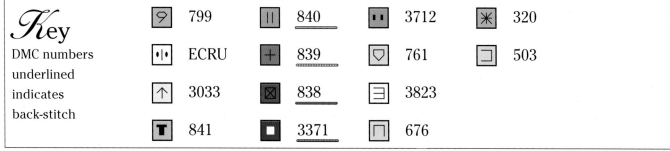

Key

DMC numbers
underlined
indicates
back-stitch

Symbol	DMC	Symbol	DMC	Symbol	DMC	Symbol	DMC
9	799	‖	840	•ı•	3712	✳	320
•ı•ı•	ECRU	+	839	▽	761	⅃	503
↑	3033	⊠	838	Ӡ	3823		
T	841	▢	3371	⊓	676		

51

Mirror

Cats are inquisitive and this adorable kitten will ensure you are not alone when scrutinizing your face in the Mirror. This Mirror will brighten up any room or hallway. If preferred, the Mirror can be placed partially behind a plant or floral decoration to enhance the plant's size and appearance.

Materials

For design, stitched area 3¼ x 4⅜ in
  (8 x 11 cm)

Piece of Zweigart 18-count Aida in Cream,
  8 x 10 in (20.5 x 25.5 cm)

DMC Stranded Embroidery Thread as follows:

838	Dark Brown
920	Dark Ginger
437	Pale Ginger
738	Pale Coffee
712	Cream
3033	Beige
453	Pale Grey
642	Pale Grey Brown
640	Medium Grey Brown
3787	Dark Grey Brown
523	Pale Sage

DMC tapestry needles, size 24

Framecraft Narrow Mirror, Model WSMW (a
Gold-finish frame is also available)

Working the cross stitch

Follow the chart, beginning in the centre of
the Aida and working outwards.

Use two strands throughout.

Finishing the work

See *Finishing Your Work* section at the end of
the book for details of fixing your stitched
work to the framing part of the mirror.

Alternative suggestions for the design

This can be framed as a picture with a mount
and a larger frame. It would also be an
attractive front cover for a small notebook,
made in the same way as the Photograph
Album Cover.

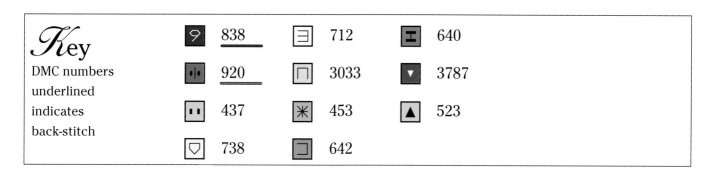

Key

DMC numbers
underlined
indicates
back-stitch

9	838	⊟	712	⊞	640
•∤•	920	⊓	3033	▼	3787
▪▪	437	✳	453	▲	523
▽	738	▨	642		

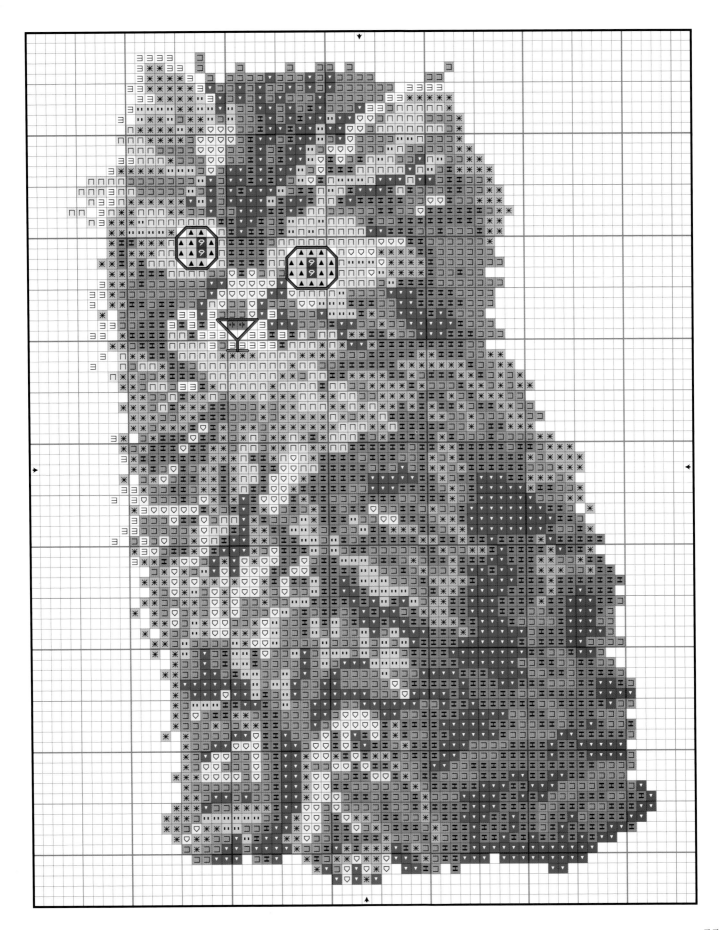

Desk Tidy

If you sometimes find it difficult to put pen
to paper, perhaps the authoritative stare of
this grey cat is just what you need to
act as a prompt!

MATERIALS

For design, stitched area 1¾ in (4.5 cm) square

Piece of Zweigart 28-count Linen in White, 7 in (18 cm) square

DMC Stranded Embroidery Thread as follows:

3820	Gold
902	Maroon
3799	Charcoal Grey
414	Dark Grey
451	Taupe
318	Blue Grey
648	Pale Stone Grey
762	Palest Grey

DMC Tapestry needles, size 24

Framecraft Wooden Desk Tidy Kit, Model WDK

WORKING THE CROSS STITCH

Follow the chart, beginning in the centre of the Linen and working outwards.

The whole design is worked using single strands of thread, but the cross stitch is worked over a single thread of the Linen, some of the back-stitch is worked over two threads and the gold edges of the book are single stitches worked across the width of the book.

FINISHING THE WORK

See *Finishing Your Work* section at the end of the book for instructions on fitting your work to a circle.

ALTERNATIVE SUGGESTION FOR THE DESIGN

This can be worked on 14- or 18-count Aida and used to decorate a box lid. If doing this, remember to allow for the increased size of fabric required.

Key

DMC numbers underlined indicates back-stitch

3820		9	3799	♥	451	▦	648
902		▪▪	414	▽	318	✳	762

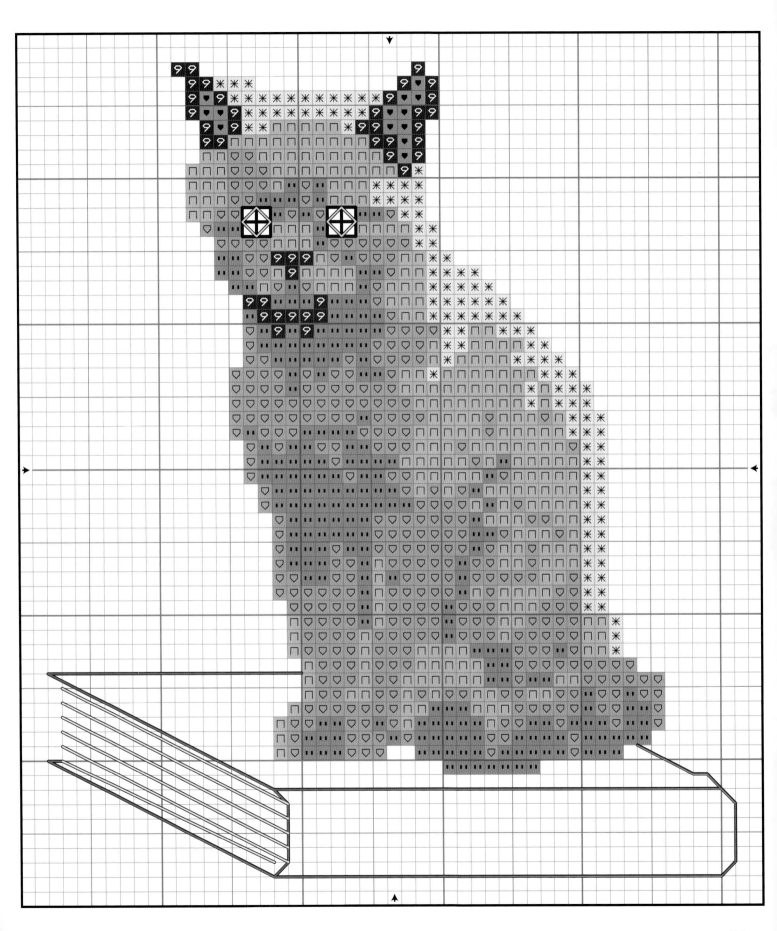

Teapot Stand

Whether you use this piece as a Teapot Stand or simply as a framed picture to prop up on a shelf, or hang on a wall, 'Ellie' will surely bring you pleasure.

MATERIALS

For design, stitched area 3⅞ x 3¾ in (10 x 9.5 cm)

Piece of Zweigart 14-count Aida in Rustico (shade 54), 10 in (25.5 cm) square

DMC Stranded Embroidery Thread as follows:

934	Darkest Green
471	Medium Green
3013	Sage Green
772	Pale Green
799	Medium Blue
341	Pale Blue
775	Palest Sky Blue
210	Mauve
407	Dusky Pink
738	Pale Orange Beige
977	Orange
3021	Dark Brown
3790	Donkey Brown
3782	Mushroom
822	Pale Mushroom
745	Palest Yellow
833	Gold

DMC Tapestry needles, size 24
Framecraft Teapot Stand, Model WTS

WORKING THE CROSS STITCH

Follow the chart, beginning in the centre of the Aida and working outwards.

Use two strands throughout.

FINISHING THE WORK

See *Finishing Your Work* section at the end of the book for instructions on fitting your work to a circle.

ALTERNATIVE SUGGESTION FOR THE DESIGN

This design can be stitched on 22-count Aida and used to decorate a box lid.

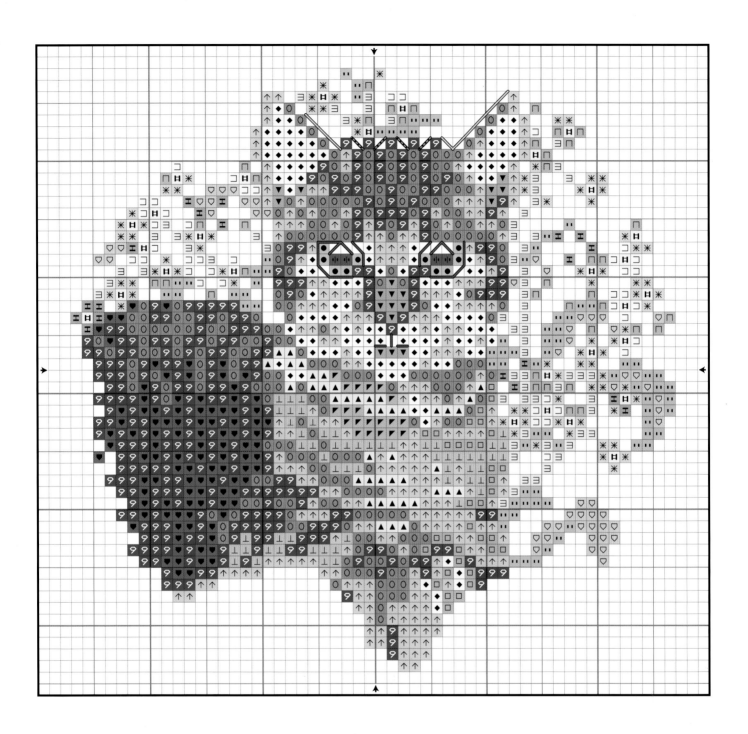

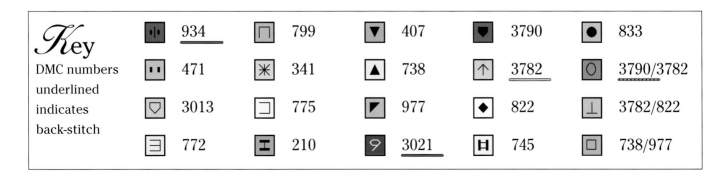

Key					
DMC numbers underlined indicates back-stitch	934	799	407	3790	833
	471	341	738	3782	3790/3782
	3013	775	977	822	3782/822
	772	210	3021	745	738/977

Picture and Cushion

This design, based on one of my own cats, Elle, can be used in two quite different ways. The cross stitch Picture uses the conventional approach, but the Cushion is easy to work as cross stitch in wool is used on large-holed canvas. Not all designs are suitable for enlargement in this way, but I hope readers will agree that the design and the added chequered border combine to make a stunning Cushion.

MATERIALS FOR FRAMED PICTURE

For design, stitched area 4¼ x 6¼ in
  (11 x 16 cm)

Piece of Zweigart 14-count Aida in Cream,
  10 x 12 in (25.5 x 31 cm)

DMC Stranded Embroidery Thread as follows:

333	Purple
349	Red
3801	Geranium Red
950	Light Pink
948	Palest Pink
727	Pale Yellow
743	Golden Yellow
742	Dark Golden Yellow
733	Olive Green
472	Pale Green
3364	Medium Green
3346	Dark Green
611	Donkey Brown
3799	Grey Black
762	Pale Grey
ECRU	Ecru
B5200	White
310	Black

DMC Tapestry needles, size 24

Picture mount, external measurement 7 x 9 in
  (18 x 23 cm)

Picture frame, internal measurement 7 x 9 in
  (18 x 23 cm)

WORKING THE CROSS STITCH

Follow the chart, beginning in the centre of
the Aida and working outwards, but stitch the
White last. Use back-stitch in 611 for the nose
and mouth, and back-stitch in 733 for the top
edge of the eye and far right daffodil.

Use three strands throughout the piece.

FINISHING THE WORK

See *Finishing Your Work* section at the end of
the book for details of preparing your work
for framing and other framing information.

MATERIALS FOR CUSHION COVER

For design, stitched area 13¾ in (35 cm) square

Piece of Zweigart Cotton Tapestry Canvas 7
  hpi double thread in White, 19 in (48 cm)
  square

DMC Tapestry Wool in the following
  quantities:

1 skein each of:

7243	Purple
7666	Red
7106	Geranium Red
7121	Light Pink
7191	Palest Pink
7078	Pale Yellow
7726	Golden Yellow
7742	Dark Golden Yellow
7677	Olive Green
7361	Pale Green
7424	Medium Green
7384	Dark Green
7525	Donkey Brown
7624	Grey Black

3 skeins 7300 Pale Grey, 6 skeins ECRU, 7
  skeins BLANC, 7 skeins NOIR

DMC Tapestry needles, size 16

Cushion backing fabric, 15 in (38 cm) square

Zip to match cushion backing fabric, 10 in
  (25.5 cm) in length

Sewing thread for attaching zip and cushion
  backing

Cushion pad, 14 in (35.5 cm)

For the tassels: 3 skeins 7666 Red, 3 skeins
  7106 Geranium Red

WORKING THE CROSS STITCH

Follow the main chart, beginning in the centre
of the canvas and working outwards. Stitch
the BLANC *after* the ECRU background. (The
ECRU background is extended by 3 rows of
cross stitch at the top edge of the design and
2 rows at the bottom edge.) Use back-stitch in
7525 for the nose and mouth, and back-stitch
in 7677 for the top edge of the eye and far
right daffodil.

  Work 1 row of 7106 at each side of the cat
design, from top to bottom.

  Work 1 row of 7666 outside the rows of
7106 at each edge of the design.

  Stitch the chequered border, as in the small
chart, on both sides of the cat.

FINISHING THE WORK

See *Finishing Your Work* section at the end of
the book for details of making up the cushion
and tassel-making.

ALTERNATIVE SUGGESTION FOR THE DESIGN

In addition to the Picture and Cushion
illustrated, the design worked on 18-count
Aida will fit into the Mirror.

Top edge of cushion strip border

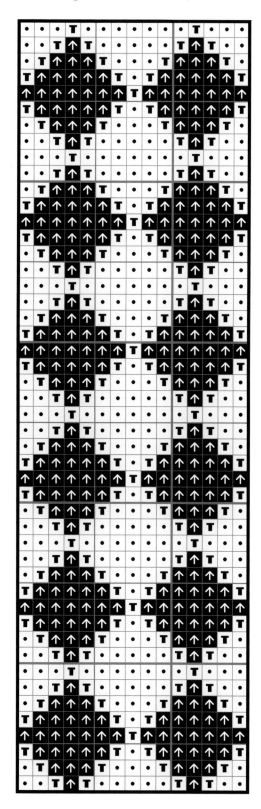

*Above: Cushion Strip Border. Repeat pattern to
bottom of cushion.*

Key

DMC numbers underlined indicates back-stitch

	Framed Picture		Cushion Cover
▪▪	333	▪▪	7243
▽	349	▽	7666
⊟	3801	⊟	7106
⊓	950	⊓	7121
✳	948	✳	7191
✕	727	✕	7078
⊣	743	⊣	7726
▼	742	▼	7742
▲	733	▲	7677
◤	472	◤	7361
▼	3364	▼	7424
◆	3346	◆	7384
●	611	●	7525
⊠	3799	⊠	7624
T	762	T	7300
•	ECRU	•	ECRU
⊐	B5200	⊐	BLANC
↑	310	↑	NOIR

Cafetière Cover

Kittens are fascinated by the world around them. This kitten was no exception and ladybirds provided endless entertainment for him. The design is repeated so that it can be viewed from both sides. However, if you only have time to stitch it once you can use the other half to add your name, or initials, or date. Whichever option you choose, this delightful kitten is bound to brighten up your coffee time.

MATERIALS

For design, stitched area of one side 4¾ x 3⅝ in (12 x 9 cm)

Piece of Zweigart 14-count Aida in Cream, 17 x 10 in (43 x 25.5 cm)

DMC Stranded Embroidery Thread as follows:

712	Pale Cream
739	Cream Beige
3827	Pale Ginger
436	Light Caramel
976	Dark Ginger
435	Dark Caramel
838	Dark Brown
817	Red
350	Geranium Red
3712	Dark Rose Pink
743	Yellow
472	Pale Green
471	Medium Green
3346	Dark Green

DMC Tapestry needles, size 24

Satin bias binding, approximately 1 yd or 1 m in Coffee or Red

Lightweight wadding, approximately 17 x 10 in (43 x 25.5 cm)

Backing fabric: Linen, Aida or Lightweight Wool, 17 x 10 in (43 x 25.5 cm)

Tacking thread

Sewing thread for bias binding and Velcro

Length of hook and loop Velcro, 10 in (25.5 cm), in a suitable colour (Pink was used in the piece illustrated)

WORKING THE CROSS STITCH

Fold the Aida in half to find the midpoint of the two design areas. Following the chart, work the design beginning at the right-hand edge of the design, four holes to the left of the centre fold. Work the repeat of the design, beginning at the left-hand edge, four holes to the right of the centre fold. (The design and repeat are therefore eight holes apart along the length of the Aida.) Work French knots in colours specified.

Five French knots in 734 on upper small strawberry
Four French knots in 734 on lower small strawberry
First ladybird: Four French knots in 838
                     Two French knots in 712
Second ladybird: Two French knots in 838
                     Two French knots in 712

Use three strands for all the cross stitch areas and one strand for all the French knots. (See Getting Started section at the beginning of the book for details of how to work French knots.)

FINISHING THE WORK

See *Finishing Your Work* section at the end of the book for details of making up your finished cover.

ALTERNATIVE SUGGESTIONS FOR THE DESIGN

A single working of the design would be suitable for: a small picture or calendar, using an oval or rectangular mount. A slightly larger picture, measuring 6 x 4½ in (15.5 x 11.5 cm) can be created by working the design on 11-count Aida. (Remember to allow for the increase in size when calculating the amount of Aida required. Remember also, that a single working of the design will be required for a picture.)

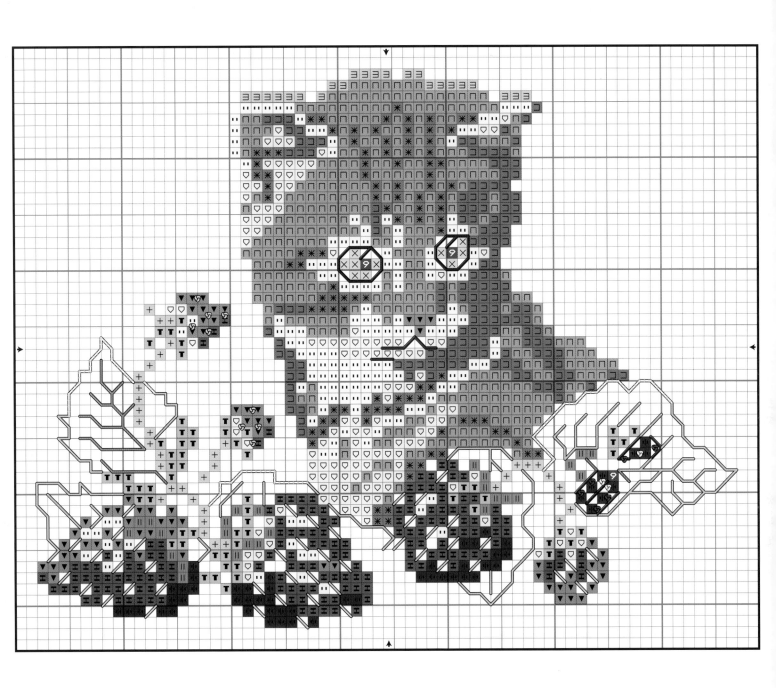

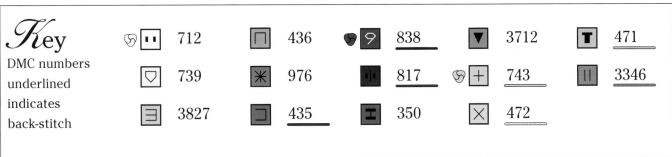

Mini-sampler

If you don't own a cat but know a person who does, then why not stitch this Mini-sampler as a gift? Alternatively, in a guest bedroom this piece will bring a smile to a visitor's face and make them feel immediately at home.

MATERIALS

For design, stitched area 5¾ x 3⅞ in
(14.5 x 10 cm)

Piece of Zweitgart 28-count Linen in Cream,
   12 x 10 in (30.5 x 25.5 cm)

DMC Stranded Embroidery Thread as follows:

310	Black
B5200	White
799	Blue
453	Pale Grey
642	Medium Grey
3787	Dark Grey
838	Dark Brown
841	Coffee
3033	Mushroom
3827	Pale Ginger
976	Ginger
349	Red
3046	Pale Gold
471	Green

DMC Tapestry needles, size 24
Framecraft Cross-over Frame, Model WCO 57

WORKING THE CROSS STITCH

Follow the chart, beginning at the centre of
the Linen and working outwards.

*Two strands are worked over two canvas
threads with the following exceptions:
'Cream' and the grey paw prints are worked in
one strand over one canvas thread.
The 'sleeping' cat's eyes and nose are worked
in one strand over one and two canvas threads.*

FINISHING THE WORK

See *Finishing Your Work* section at the end of
the book for details of preparing your work
for framing and other framing information.

ALTERNATIVE SUGGESTIONS FOR THE DESIGN

Various elements of the sampler can be used
to decorate small items. For example, you can
make a set of cat buttons to personalize a
cardigan or jacket.

Key
DMC numbers
underlined
indicates
back-stitch

9 310	T 453	⊠ 838	◆ 3827	▲ 3046
·ı· B5200	‖ 642	⊠ 841	O 976	▼ 471
↑ 799	⊠ 3787	■ 3033	▪▪ 349	

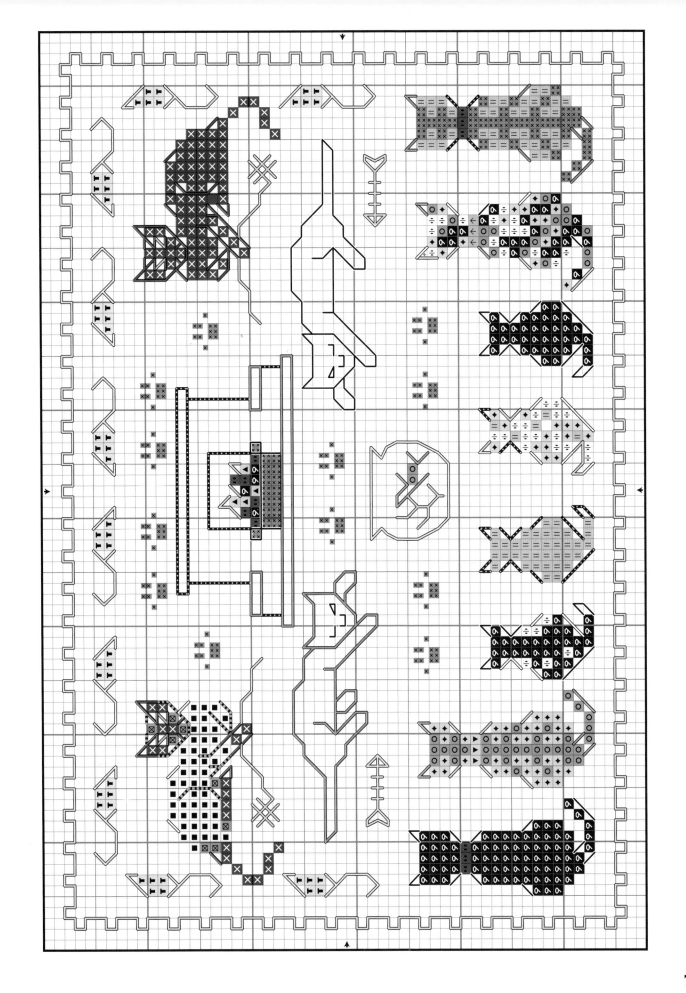

Plant Mat

On a sunny day cats often like to hide in a cool spot, *after* sunbathing of course, and ivy provides one perfect cover. This has been designed for use as a mat for a plant on a low-level table. However, it can also be used on a shelf with the triangular design overhanging the shelf edge.

MATERIALS

For design, stitched area 8⅜ in (21.5 cm) square

Piece of Zweigart 14-count Aida in White, 9¾ in (24.5 cm) square

DMC Stranded Embroidery Thread as follows:

760	Dark Pink
453	Mink
948	Pale Pink
762	Pale Grey
648	Medium Grey
646	Dark Grey
844	Mud
935	Darkest Green
987	Dark Green
3347	Medium Green
472	Lime green
834	Gold
3823	Cream
BLANC	White

DMC Tapestry needles, size 24
Satin bias binding, 40 in (1 m), in Dark Green
Sewing cotton to match bias binding

WORKING THE CROSS STITCH

Prior to commencing the cross stitch, attach the bias binding to construct the mat. Begin and end the bias binding at one corner of the Aida. You will probably find that you have three rounded corners and one square corner. Begin the cross stitch in the corner opposite the square corner. The corner cross stitch will be seven rows in from the inside of each edge of the bias binding, counted from the inner edges of the binding.

Follow the chart, working the cat first and then each of the ivy sprigs.

Use two strands for the cat and ivy leaves and one strand for the back-stitch outlining the leaves.

FINISHING THE WORK

Press with a damp cloth and a medium heat iron on the reverse side of the fabric.

ALTERNATIVE SUGGESTIONS FOR THE DESIGN

This design can be worked on an oblong piece of fabric to create a tray cloth. For this use, the design should be worked in two opposite corners. Another idea is to use it for the Square Tray.

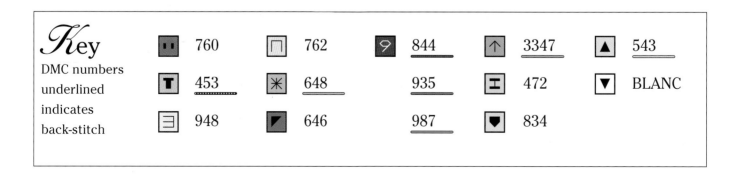

Key
DMC numbers underlined indicates back-stitch

760		762		844		3347		543	
453		648		935		472		BLANC	
948		646		987		834			

80

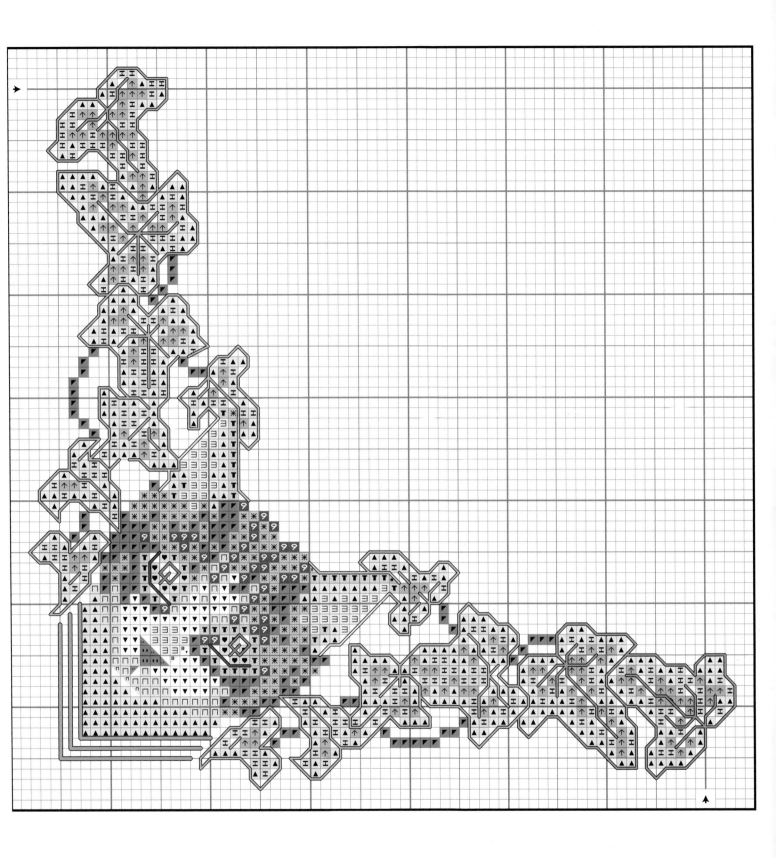

Photograph Album Cover

This design uses the half-Persian cat featured in the Wooden Needles and Scissors Box. The border is intentionally simple so that it can be extended or adapted to accommodate different sizes of photograph album. Alternatively, you can use it to cover a diary, sketch book, or other small book.

MATERIALS

For design, stitched area 5½ x 3¾ in (14 x 9.5 cm)

Piece of Zweigart 14-count Aida in Black, 9 x 15 in (23 x 38 cm)

DMC Crewel Embroidery Wool as follows:

BLANC	White
8739	Buttermilk
8846	Pale Ginger
8845	Ginger
8301	Dark Ginger
8166	Dusky Pink
8742	Gold
8420	Green

DMC Tapestry needles, size 22

Black sewing cotton

Photograph Album

Double-sided adhesive tape

WORKING THE CROSS STITCH

Begin with either the tip of the cat's tail or the bottom left-hand corner or the green border, commencing your stitching ½ in (1.5 cm) from what will be the corner of the book. To find where the corner will be on the Aida, wrap the fabric round the book like a loose-leaf cover, ensuring that both ends tucked inside the album's front and back covers are similar in length. Also check that you have the other two edges matching each other in length. Find the bottom left-hand corner and mark with either chalk or a pin. Remove the Aida from the book and commence stitching ½ in (1.5 cm) from the pin in both up and across directions.

Use one strand of Crewel Embroidery Wool throughout.

FINISHING THE WORK

Photograph albums vary in size so you will need to adapt the cover to your particular album as follows:

Place the stitched area in the centre of the front cover. Wrap the rest of the fabric round the back of the album. Trim the edges which will form the 'pockets' for the album so that you have 2 in (5 cm) for the inside of each cover end. Trim the other edges which are at right-angles to the 'pockets' allowing ⅜ in (1 cm) for each hem. Use double-sided tape for these edges and fold under to create a neat edge. To make the 'pockets', turn the edges under ⅜ in (1 cm), then turn again to create a 'pocket' approximately 1½ in (3.5 cm) deep. Slip stitch to secure the edges of the 'pockets'. Fit to the album.

ALTERNATIVE SUGGESTIONS FOR THE DESIGN

Apart from the suggestion for this design made in the Wooden Needles and Scissors Box, it can also be used as a repeat motif for the Calico Bag panel. It can either be worked three times with suitable spacing, or twice in the space, reversing one of the motifs, so that you have two cats looking at each other.

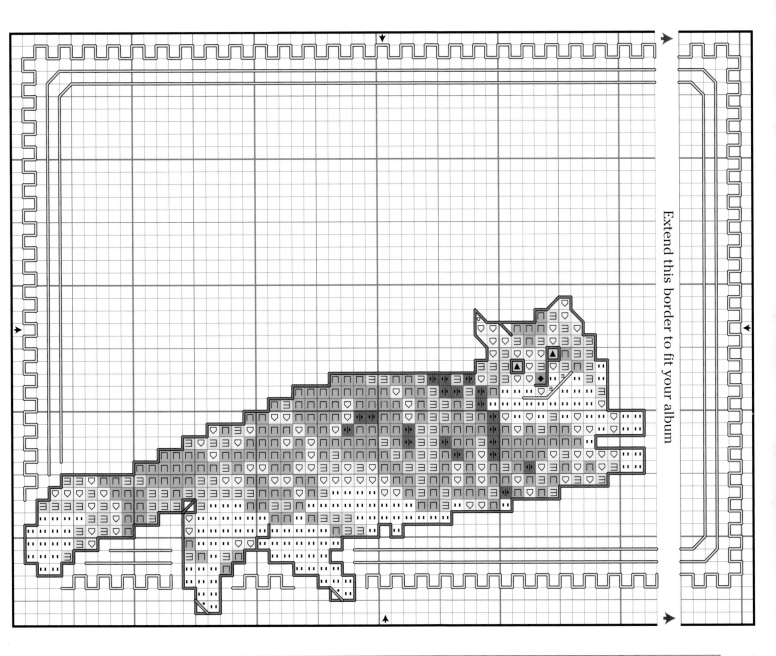

Extend this border to fit your album

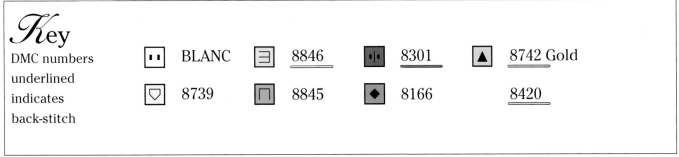

$\mathcal{K}$ey

DMC numbers
underlined
indicates
back-stitch

▫ BLANC	∃ 8846	◈ 8301	▲ 8742 Gold
▽ 8739	⊓ 8845	◆ 8166	8420

Wall-hanging

Juliet is not quite on a balcony but she is fond
of sitting in a variety of inappropriate containers
– everything from a laundry basket to the
hanging basket shown here. Like most cats she
prefers to rest in a discarded cardboard box
rather than a specially designed cat bed.

MATERIALS

For design, stitched area 4¼ x 7⅝ in
  (11 x 19.5 cm)

Piece of Zweigart 14-count Aida in White,
  9 x 15 in (23 x 38 cm)

DMC Stranded Embroidery Thread as follows:

310	Black
3799	Charcoal
762	Pale Grey
BLANC	White
3823	Cream
3820	Gold
3772	Pinky Brown
758	Blush
951	Flesh
957	Pink
892	Pink Red
553	Violet
340	Bluebell
113	Variegated Blue
3053	Sage Green
703	Bright Green
472	Lime Green
470	Green
831	Moss

DMC Tapestry needles, size 24
Framecraft Bell-pull ends, Model WBP5
Iron-on backing fabric
Double-sided adhesive tape for fixing hems

WORKING THE CROSS STITCH

Follow the chart, beginning in the centre of the Aida and working outwards.

Use two strands throughout.

FINISHING THE WORK

Carefully iron the back of your work to remove all creases. Use a medium-hot iron and a damp cloth. Place the iron-on backing fabric in position on the back of your work, adhesive side down, and iron. Leave to cool on the ironing board. When cool, trim the finished piece to size, remembering to leave ⅜ in (1 cm) for each side hem and 1 in (2.5 cm) top and bottom for the bell-pull ends. Fix double-sided tape to the side edges and make a hem. Do the same at the top and bottom edges but create a hem 2 in (5 cm) deep, leaving space to slide the bell-pull ends into position.

ALTERNATIVE SUGGESTIONS FOR THE DESIGN

This can be framed as a picture. If you want to do something more elaborate, then why not use it as a centre panel for a small cushion?

Key
DMC numbers underlined indicates back-stitch

Symbol	DMC	Symbol	DMC	Symbol	DMC	Symbol	DMC	Symbol	DMC
☒	310	✳	3823	●	951	■	340	▲	472
⊠	3799	⬚	3820	H	957	▲	113	◪	470
←	762	→	3772	T	892	⬈	3053	▲	831
⬚	BLANC		758	♥	553	△	703		

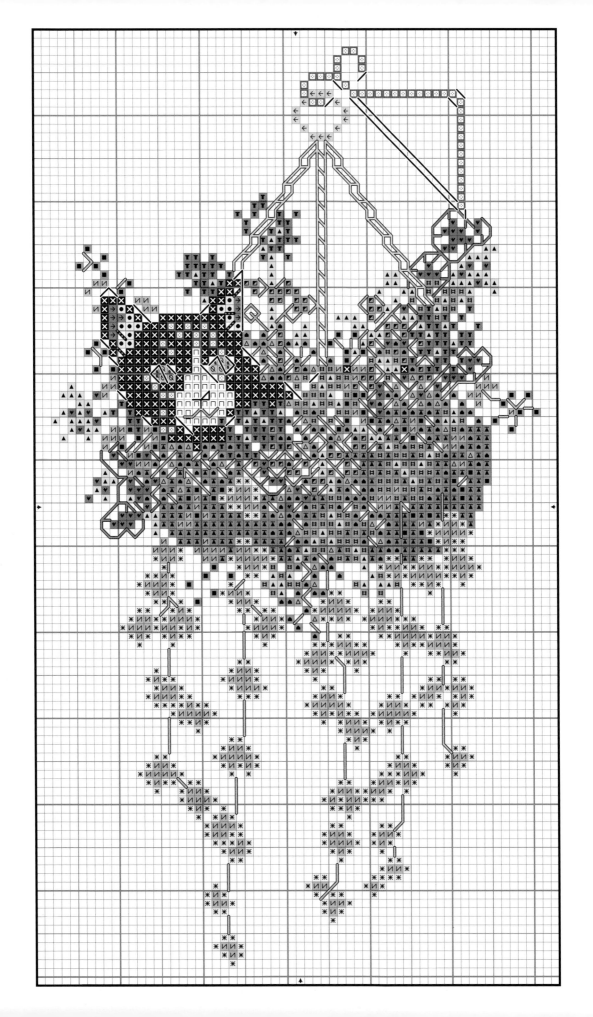

Calico Bag

This bag can be used for a variety of purposes,
but if you need something in which to store
used polythene bags this is ideal. The rainbow's
colours have been used for the design so that it
will fit in with most kitchen colour schemes.
Of course, it can always be used to carry
home your cat's food shopping!

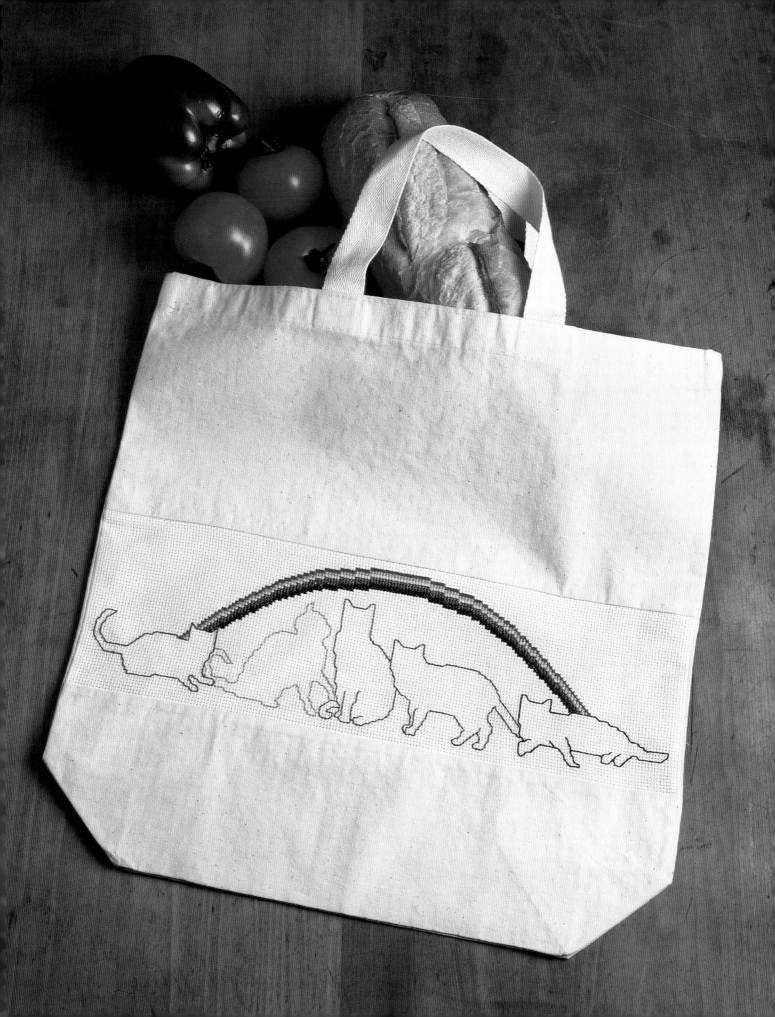

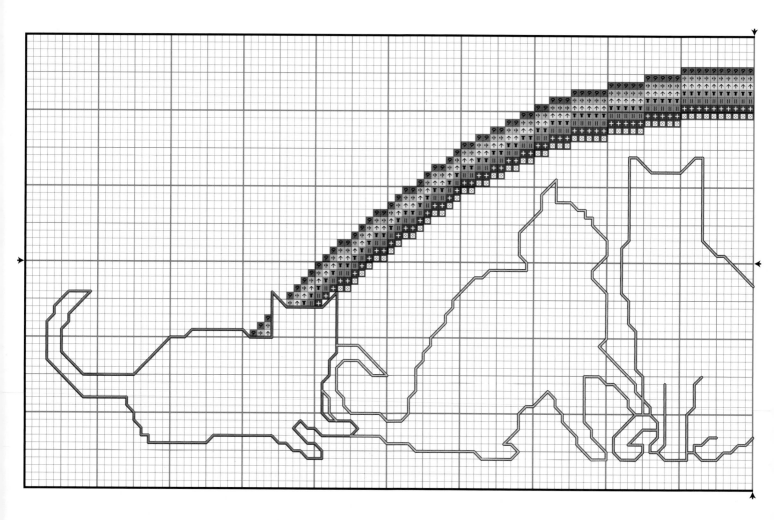

MATERIAL

*For design, stitched area 13½ x 3¾ in
(34.5 x 9.5 cm)*

Framecraft Calico bag with Aida insert, Model
TBAGE

DMC Stranded Embroidery Thread as follows:

606	Red
741	Orange
726	Yellow
905	Green
798	Blue
791	Indigo
550	Violet

DMC Tapestry needles, size 24

WORKING THE CROSS STITCH

Find the mid-point of the Aida panel and
commence the mid-point of the rainbow on
this line, leaving three clear rows of Aida from
the top edge of the panel to the first stitch of
the red in the rainbow.

Use two strands throughout.

FINISHING THE WORK

Iron the bag, inside out, using a damp cloth
and a medium-hot iron.

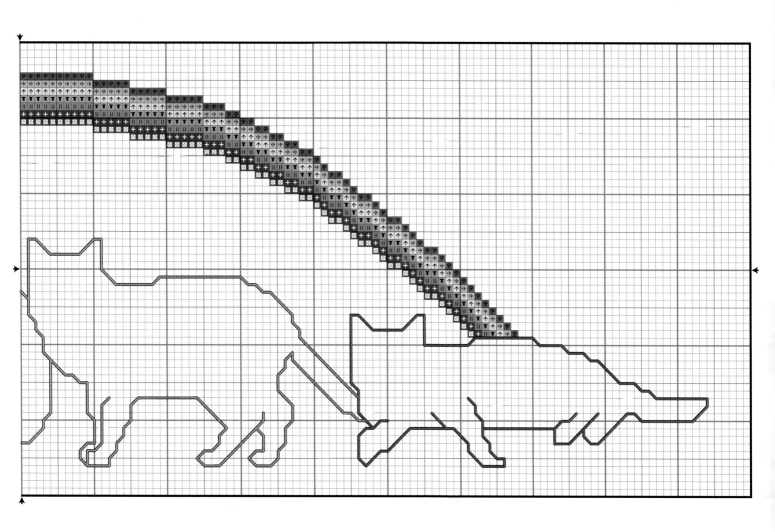

ALTERNATIVE SUGGESTIONS FOR THE DESIGN

This can be framed and would brighten up a nursery or a child's bedroom. Alternatively, the individual cat outlines can be used to decorate a variety of small items.

Key
DMC numbers underlined indicates back-stitch

Symbol	DMC	Symbol	DMC
9	606	II	798
•|•	741	+	791
↑	726	⊠	550
T	905		

Clock

These three rescued cats all have an owner in common but there is no reason why you cannot substitute your own cat or cats for any or all of those in the design of this pretty clock.

MATERIALS

For design, stitched area 4¼ x 6⅛ in (11 x 15.5 cm)

Piece of Zweigart 14-count Aida in White, 10 x 14 in (25.5 x 35.5 cm)

DMC Stranded Embroidery Thread as follows:

310	Black
3799	Dark Grey
3371	Dark Brown
3021	Medium Brown
746	Cream
BLANC	White
3779	Pink
972	Orange Yellow
444	Dark Yellow
727	Lemon
3348	Lime Green
368	Pale Apple Green
320	Apple Green
964	Turquoise Green
825	Kingfisher Blue
792	Bluebell
3746	Mauve
209	Pale Violet
552	Violet

DMC Tapestry needles, size 24
Framecraft Clock, Model WS Mantel
French Navy Aerosol Spray Paint

WORKING THE CROSS STITCH

The small circle of back-stitch at the centre of the clock should be stitched first. Follow the chart and work outwards from this area.

Use two strands throughout.

FINISHING THE WORK

See *Finishing Your Work* section at the end of the book for details of preparing your work for framing. Spray the Clock with thin coats of spray paint, allowing 24 hours between coats. Then follow the instructions provided with the clock for completing the project.

ALTERNATIVE SUGGESTIONS FOR THE DESIGN

The central design can be used for a box top or to decorate the front of a covered book, such as the Photograph Album Cover.

If you wish to substitute another cat's face for one in the design you will need a photograph of the face which is similar in size to that in the design. Lay a piece of 14 squares per inch design paper over the top and trace the outline on to the paper. Fill in the detail from your photograph and then stitch.

Key

DMC numbers underlined indicates back-stitch

9	310	⊟	746	⏍	444	H	320	◤	3746
‖	3799	⊓	BLANC	▼	727	T	964	◣	209
▪▪	3371	⦙	3779	◆	3348	∧	825	+	552
▽	3021	✳	972	●	368	▲	792		

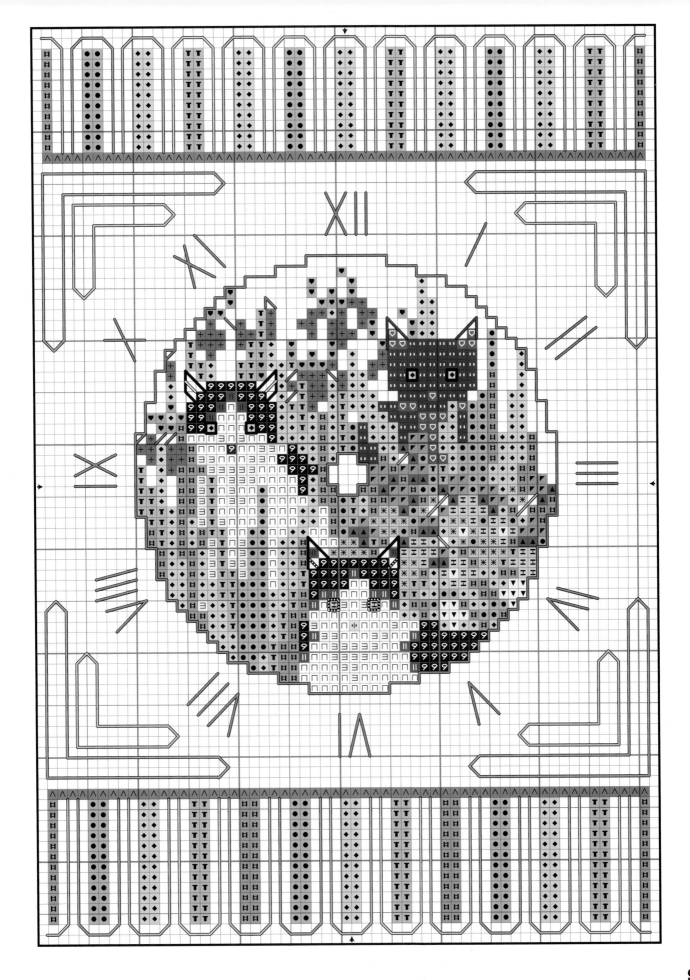

Square Tray

$Penny$ is special and she loves her garden. However, using the technique described in the previous project, you can substitute your own cat's face in the centre of the design.

MATERIALS

For design, stitched area 8 in (20.5 cm) square

Piece of Zweigart 28-count Linen in White,
    15 in (38 cm) square

DMC Stranded Embroidery Thread as follows:

The Cat

BLANC	White
677	Buttermilk
676	Dark Cream
111	Variegated Gold
422	Coffee
436	Pale Ginger
613	Fawn
3787	Mud Grey
844	Charcoal Grey
310	Black
3778	Pink

The Nasturtiums

94	Variegated Green
3827	Blush
745	Pale Yellow
743	Yellow
741	Orange
947	Dark Orange
349	Red

DMC Tapestry needles, size 24
Framecraft Square Tray, Model WSST

WORKING THE CROSS STITCH

Work the first corner motif 3½ in (9 cm) from
the corner of the Linen. Work each corner
motif in turn, rotating the chart through 90°
and leaving 15 stitches between the edges of
the motifs. (15 stitches = 30 threads of the
Linen.)

Work the cat's face by finding the centre of
your fabric and working from the centre of
the chart.

Use two strands throughout.

FINISHING THE WORK

See *Finishing Your Work* section at the end of
the book for details of preparing your work for
framing. Then follow the instructions provided
with the tray to complete the project.

ALTERNATIVE SUGGESTIONS FOR THE DESIGN

The corner motif can be used for a tray cloth
or napkins. The cat's face can be used to
decorate either a teapot stand or, if stitched
on 18-count Aida, for a box top.

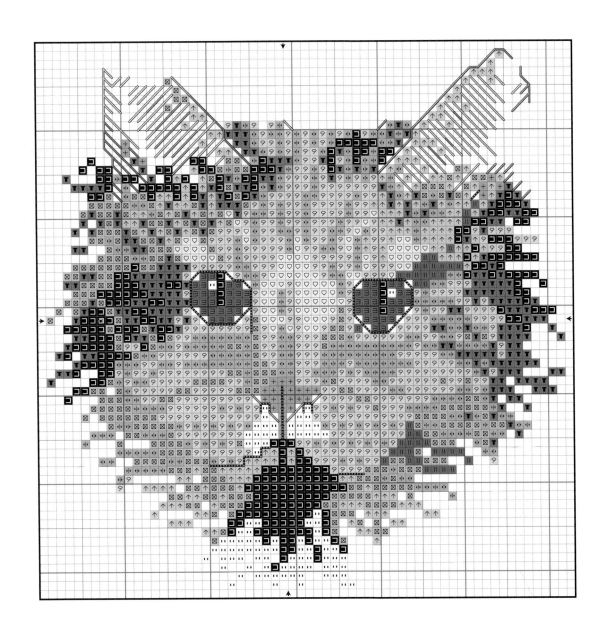

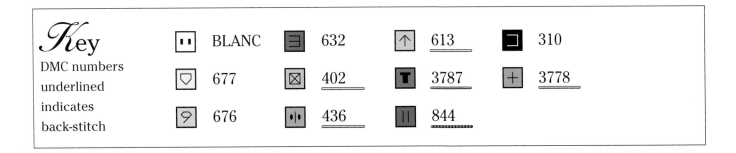

Key

DMC numbers
underlined
indicates
back-stitch

⊡	BLANC
▽	677
⌐	676
⊟	632
⊠	402
◖▮◗	436
↑	613
T	3787
‖	844
⊐	310
+	3778

Above: Key for Cat

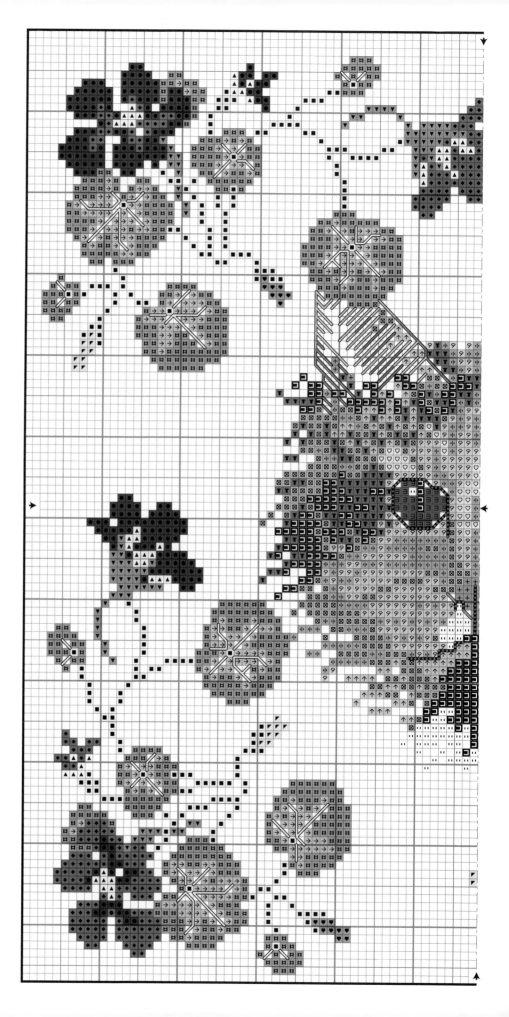

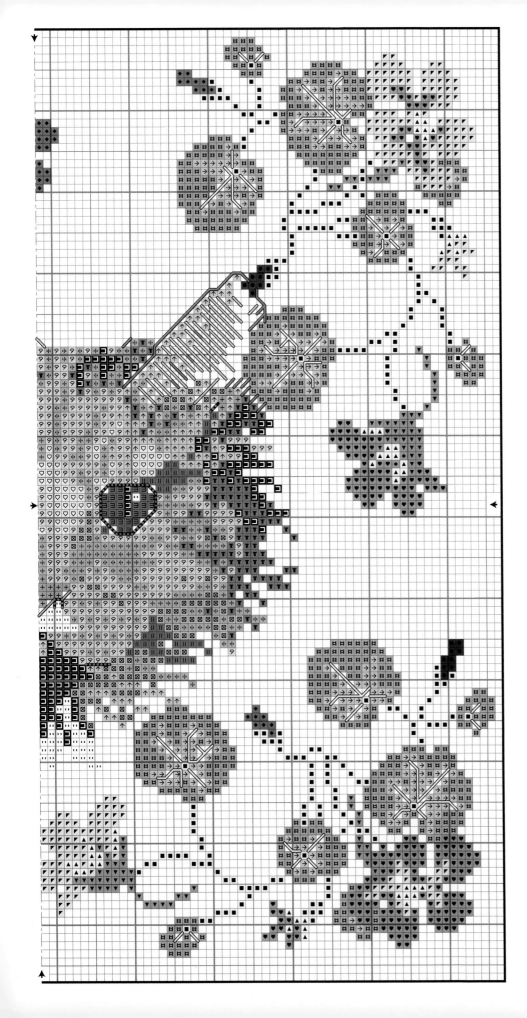

Key

DMC numbers
underlined
indicates
back-stitch

■	<u>471</u>
→	472
H	520
▲	745
◤	743
▼	741
▽	783
◆	947
■	349

*Above: Key for
Nasturtiums*

Oval Tray

Misty and Softy are glamorous cats who love
to lie around looking decorative. They enjoy
'gardening', which is better described as lazing
in the sunny flower borders, and so are a
suitable pair for this elegant floral tray. This tray
has been created as a 'thank you' for a couple
who are good neighbours but it would also be a
suitable birthday gift or retirement present,
especially as the tray can be purchased
with a presentation box.

MATERIALS

For design, stitched area 11⅝ x 6¾ in (30 x 17 cm)

Piece of Zweigart 25-count Dublin Linen in Shade 222, 18 x 13 in (46 x 33 cm)

DMC Stranded Embroidery Thread as follows:

645	Dark Grey
647	Stone Grey
648	Grey
3072	Pale Grey
BLANC	White
760	Pink
335	Red
436	Pale Brown
834	Antique Gold
727	Yellow
472	Lime Green
471	Green
3012	Olive Green
504	Pale Turquoise
340	Mauve

DMC Tapestry needles, size 24

Framecraft Wood Oval Tray, Model WOT (or PWOT if the presentation box is required)

WORKING THE CROSS STITCH

Follow the chart, beginning in the centre of the Linen and working outwards.

Use three strands for everything except the gold border and stripes background, for which one strand is used.

FINISHING THE WORK

Follow the manufacturer's instructions for assembling the tray.

Key

DMC numbers underlined indicates backstitch

⑨	645	⊟	3072	✳	335	▼	727	▼	3012
▪▪	647	⊓	BLANC	⊒	436	▲	472	◆	504
▽	648	•ı•	760	⊐	834	◤	471	●	340

Above: Key for Embroidery Thread

ALTERNATIVE SUGGESTION FOR THE DESIGN

This design can be adapted in the way that the black and white cat Picture has been used to create a companion Cushion. Extending the stripes and adding a background colour, the design can be worked on 10 hpi Tapestry Canvas (double thread would be best) in half-cross stitch using wool. It will make a rectangular cushion measuring 16 x 12 in (40.5 x 30.5 cm). The recommended DMC Tapestry Wool colours are as follows:

7275	Dark Grey
7273	Stone Grey
7618	Grey
7282	Pale Grey
BLANC	White
7105	Pink
7104	Red
7846	Pale Brown
7473	Antique Gold
7078	Yellow
7584	Lime Green
7583	Green
7364	Olive Green
7322	Pale Turquoise
7711	Mauve
7746	Cream for the background

Tapestry needles, size 16

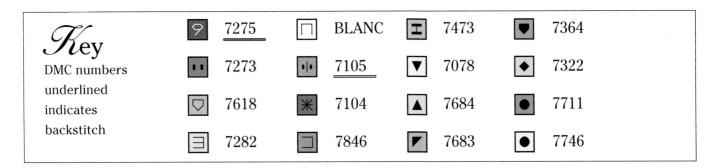

Above: Key for Tapestry Wool

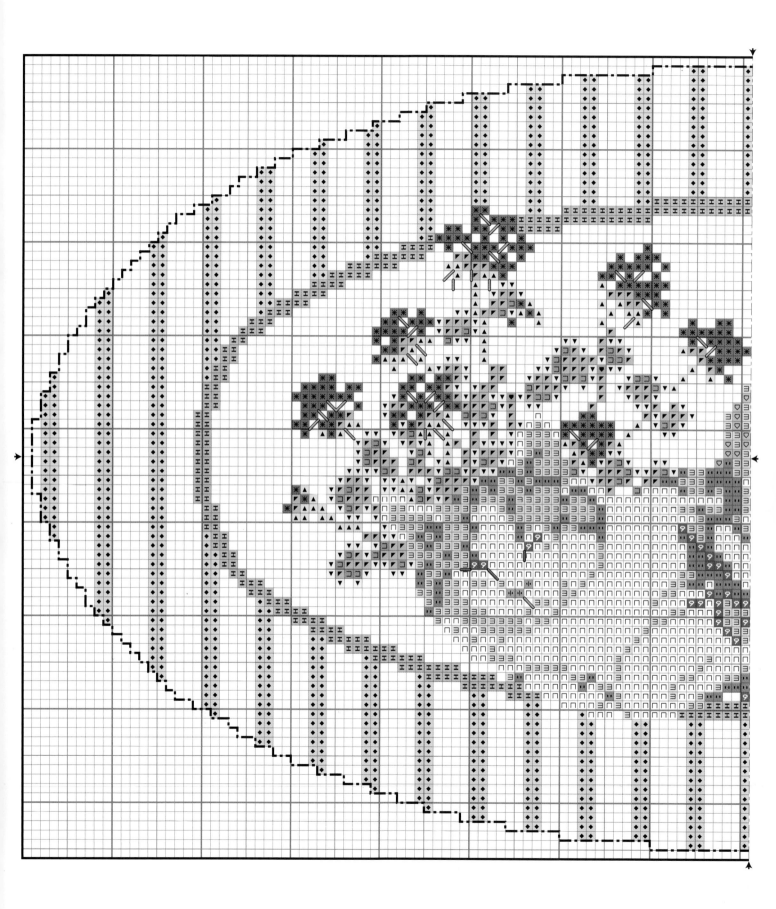

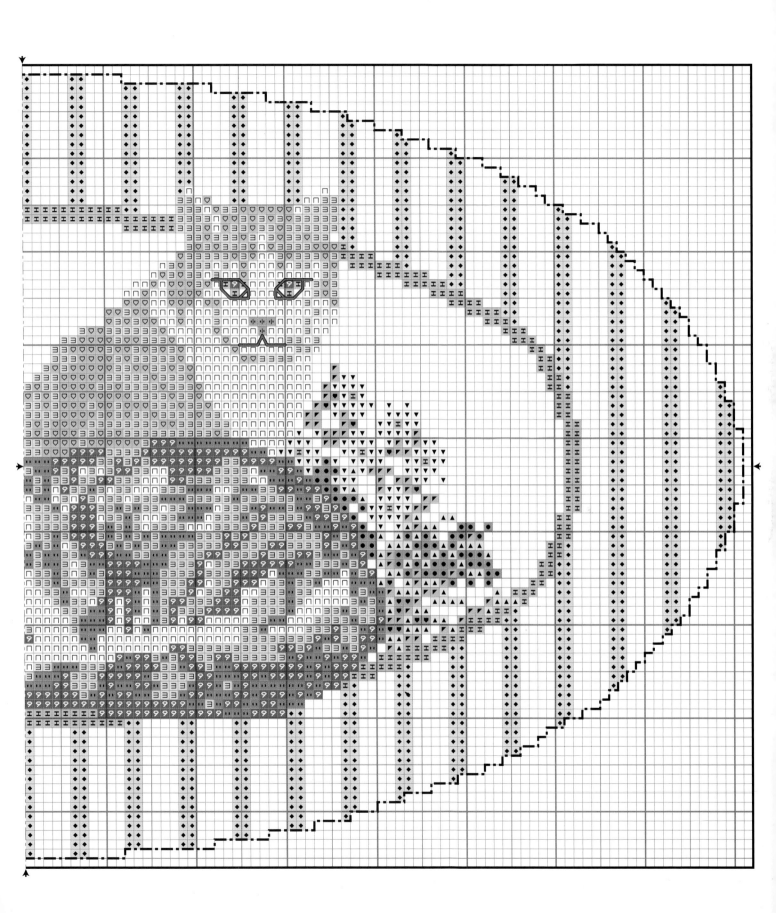

Herb Pillow

This long-haired kitten is the same design as used for the Mirror but is worked in a different colourway. It is also worked on larger-holed fabric and, combined with the tartan background it makes a very pretty Herb Pillow. The bottom edge is left open and secured with ribbons so that the herbs can easily be renewed. The colours of the tartan background can easily be substituted, if desired, with shades to complement the colours of your room.

MATERIALS

For design, stitched area 8½ in (21.5 cm) square

Piece of Zweigart 14-count Aida in Blue Shade 589, 14 x 28 in (35.5 x 71 cm)

DMC Stranded Embroidery Thread as follows:

310	Black
353	Pink
422	Pale Gold
739	Pale Coffee
B5200	White
746	Rich Cream
712	Milk
822	Stone
3033	Pale Mushroom
3782	Mushroom
799	Blue
501	Sea Green
989	Green
666	Red

DMC Tapestry needles, size 24
Sewing thread to match the Aida and Ribbon
Length of Blue Ribbon (to match 799), 60 in (150 cm)
Wadding
Herbs

WORKING THE CROSS STITCH

Along the two short edges press under a hem allowance of ⅝ in (1.5 cm). Slip stitch both hems. Fold the fabric in half to create the pillow shape. Find the centre of the front half and work the chart beginning in the centre and working outwards.

Use three strands for the cat and two strands for the tartan and the back stitch.

FINISHING THE WORK

Stitch the side seams of the pillow, right sides together, using the ⅝ in (1.5 cm) seam allowance. Turn rightside out and press the back of the pillow and the side seams using a damp cloth and warm iron. Cut the ribbon into four equal lengths and attach the ribbons, approximately one quarter the pillow width in from each edge, to the back and front bottom edges of the pillow. Fold the wadding in half so that it fits the pillow and insert the herbs in the fold. Place in the pillow so that the folded edge is at the bottom edge of the pillow. Tie the ribbons to secure the wadding in place.

ALTERNATIVE SUGGESTIONS FOR THE DESIGN

The tartan pattern can be applied to a whole range of items and the colours can be changed to match different settings. The kitten makes a pretty picture in its own right.

Below: Key for Kitten

Key

DMC numbers underlined indicates back-stitch

🕃	310	▽	739	✳	712	▼	3782
	353	⊟	B5200	⊐	822	▲	799
	422	⊓	746	⊡	3033		

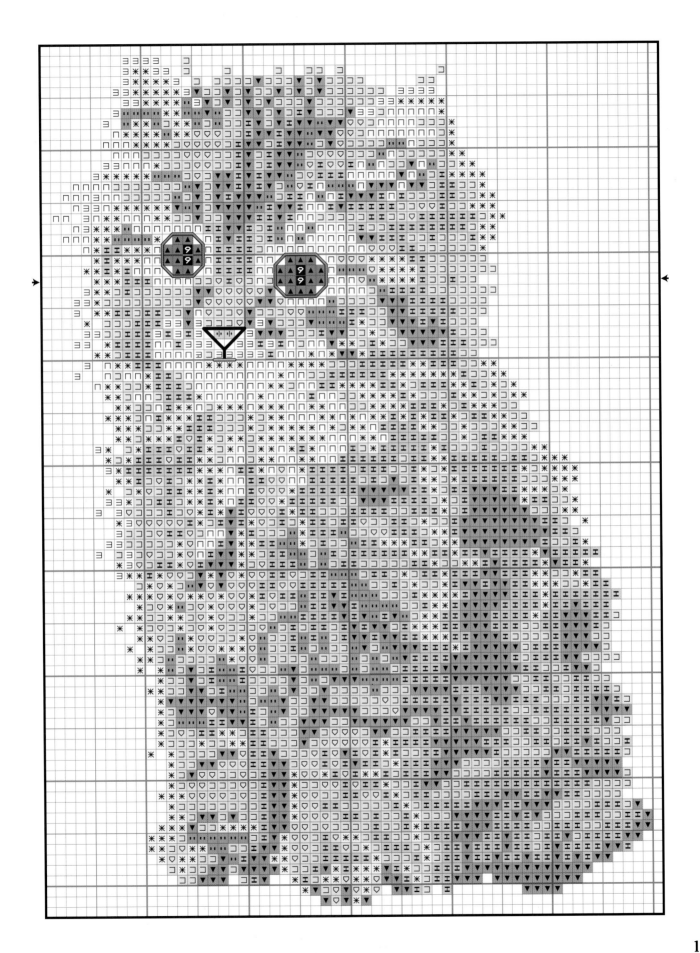

113

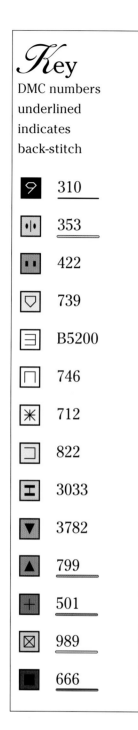

Key

DMC numbers
underlined
indicates
back-stitch

Symbol	Number
9	<u>310</u>
◐|◐	<u>353</u>
▪▪	422
▽	739
目	B5200
⊓	746
✳	712
⊐	822
H	3033
▼	3782
▲	<u>799</u>
+	<u>501</u>
⊠	<u>989</u>
■	<u>666</u>

Above: Key for
Background

114

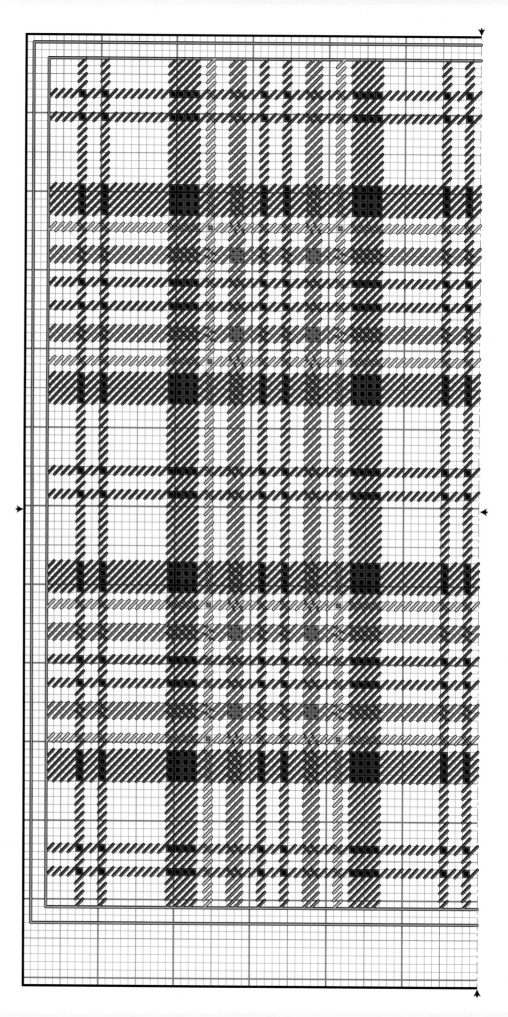

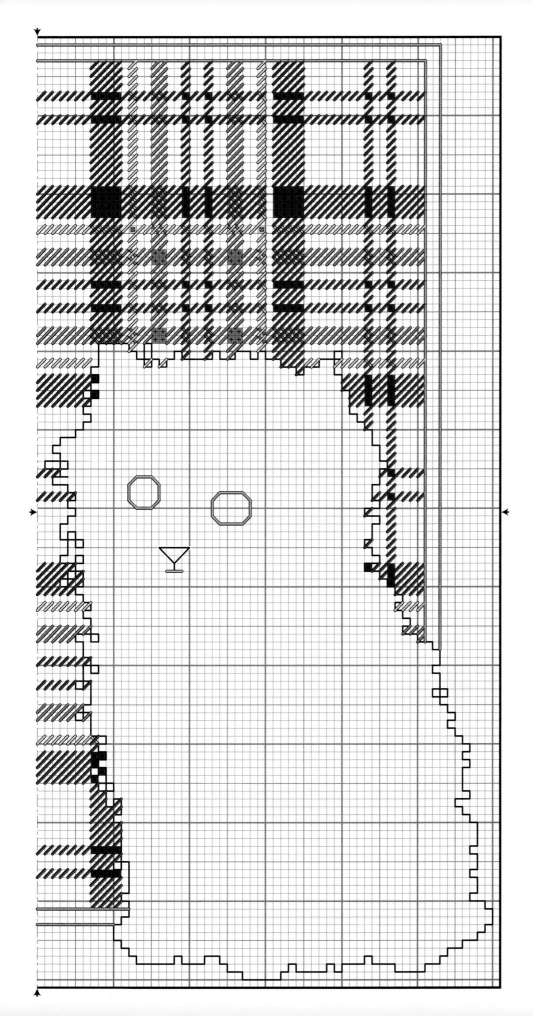

Breakfast Set

Breakfast is not everyone's favourite moment of the day so this cheery trio should put a smile on your face. The gingham border is worked in red but would look equally good in green, yellow or blue, so it can be adapted for individual breakfast room/kitchen colour schemes. The kittens are reduced in size for the egg cosies simply by stitching the same chart on finer fabric. Make as many egg cosies as you need and to make each one distinctive, vary the colour of the single poppy on the reverse side of the cosy.

MATERIALS

For tea cosy, stitched area 12½ x 9¾ in (32 x 25 cm) and egg cosy, stitched area 3¾ x 4⅞ in (9.5 x 12.5 cm)

Piece of Zweigart 11-count Aida in Antique White, 18 x 14 in (46 x 36 cm) for the tea cosy

Two pieces of Zweigart 14-count Aida in Antique White, 6½ x 8 in (16.5 x 20.5 cm) for each egg cosy

DMC Stranded Embroidery Thread as follows:

310	Black
414	Dark Grey
3024	Pale Grey
BLANC	White
727	Pale Yellow
972	Yellow
741	Pale Orange
608	Orangey Red
666	Red
304	Dark Red
353	Pink
3827	Pale Ginger
3776	Ginger
3782	Brown
3787	Bronze
472	Lime Green
3347	Green

DMC Tapestry needles, size 24

Wadding, lining and backing fabric for the tea cosy

Wadding and lining for the egg cosies

Sewing thread

Bias binding in Red to match the gingham border

Air-soluble pen

Below: Key for Back of Egg Cosy

WORKING THE CROSS STITCH

Follow the charts, beginning in the centre of the Aida and working outwards.

Use three strands for the tea cosy and two strands for the egg cosies.

FINISHING THE WORK

Following the curved shape indicated on the charts, and using an air-soluble pen, mark the top edge of the cosy. Make a 'sandwich' of the layers as follows:

> Cosy front, right side up
> Wadding
> Two pieces of lining fabric
> Wadding
> Cosy back, right side down

Tack the pieces ready for stitching. Stitch through all the layers commencing at the side edge of the gingham border and continue round to the other edge following your marked line and leaving the bottom edge open. Trim the seam to ¼ in (0.6 cm) and attach the bias binding to the seam stitching. If you wish to add a ribbon loop at the centre top of the cosies, position one end in place adding it to the 'sandwich'. Attach the other end when hemming the bias binding. Attach bias binding to the bottom edge of the cosy so that the binding is at the bottom edge of the gingham pattern. Trim the seam and hem the binding.

ALTERNATIVE SUGGESTIONS FOR THE DESIGN

The kitten images can be used for greetings cards as can the central area with the adult cat. It can also be adapted to make an attractive picture if stitched on 18-count Aida.

𝒦ey
DMC numbers underlined indicates backstitch

✳ 727	⊏ 741	⊡ 3787	⊤ 3347
⊐ 972	■ 666	H 472	

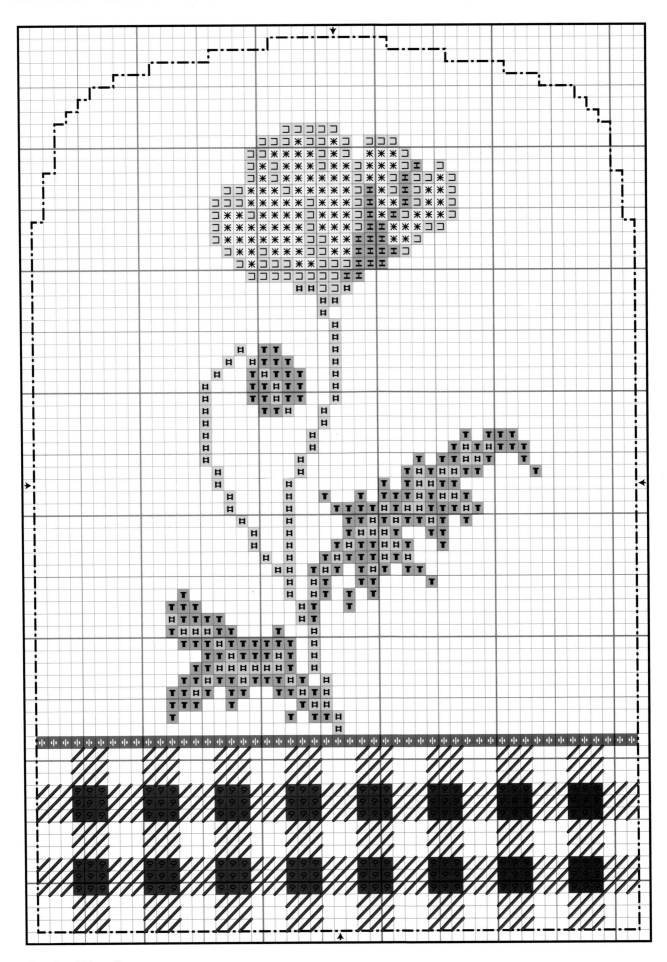

Back of Egg Cosy

Key

DMC numbers underlined indicates back-stitch

Symbol	DMC
⊞	<u>310</u>
▽	414
⊟	712
⊓	BLANC
✳	727
⊐	972
⊞	741
▼	<u>608</u>
ᧇ	<u>666</u>
▲	304
◪	<u>353</u>
▼	3827
◆	3776
●	3782
⬗	<u>3787</u>
H	472
T	3347

*Left: Tea Cosy and
Front of Egg Cosy*

Finishing Your Work

Remove your finished piece from the hoop or frame if you have used one. Trim any excess lengths of thread you may have left at the back of your stitching. Examine the unstitched areas and check they have remained clean. If they have not, use a sachet of specially-formulated detergent, available from most good needlework shops, and wash your work following the manufacturer's instructions. When it is dry, carefully iron the reverse side of your work using a damp cloth and a medium-hot iron. Trim the fabric to the required size (see further information below).

FITTING WORK TO AN OVAL

(Greetings Cards, Address Book, Wooden Needles and Scissors Box)

An easy way to do this is to use a piece of tracing paper as a guide. Cut a piece of tracing paper to fit the card, book or oval area to be covered. When in position, trace with pencil the outline of the oval. Remove the tracing paper and place it over your stitched pieces, locating the design in the centre of the drawn oval. Pin to the fabric and trim the fabric to fit the paper. Remove the pins and fit to the finished item. For the Greetings Card, use double-sided adhesive tape to secure the item in position. For the Address Book, carefully slide the work into position in the front cover. For the Wooden Needles and Scissors Box, use double-sided tape to secure

the fabric to the back of the cardboard insert and then again use tape to secure it to the top of the box. (See the section below for creating a second oval – or circle.)

FITTING WORK TO A CIRCLE

(Paperweight, Silver-plated Box, Desk Tidy, Teapot Stand)

Use the same approach with tracing paper described above but bear in mind that the circle you draw will most likely be the size of your finished item. You can still use this to centralize the design but will need to draw another circle outside this as a guide for trimming the fabric to a circular shape. (A plate or saucer can be used for this purpose.) Remember to leave sufficient fabric to tuck under the lid or backing of the Silver-plated Box, the Desk Tidy and the Teapot Stand. The Paperweight will not have any hem or fabric to tuck behind and will need to be cut to the exact size of the Paperweight's inner edge. Full manufacturer's instructions are provided for the fitting of the work to each of the purchased items.

PREPARING WORK FOR FRAMING

(Calendar, Candlescreen, Mirror, Clock, Square Tray, Mini-sampler)

All the above projects can be prepared for framing using the following method. However, for the Clock full instructions are provided with the purchased clock kit.

Use the same approach with tracing paper as described in *Fitting Work to an Oval*, above, but make the paper the same size as the backing board. Do not trim the fabric at this stage. Use the paper to locate the design in the appropriate place, in the case of the Calendar remembering to leave space for fixing the calendar blank. Pin the paper to the design. Place the fabric on to the board, matching the edges of the paper to the edges of the board. You can either begin to secure the fabric to the board by placing pins into the top and bottom edges of the board or by using double-sided adhesive tape fixed to the back of the board. After securing the top and bottom edges, continue to use the fabric threads as a guide to securing the side edges. If you find the fabric at the back of the board is a little bulky, you can trim it. Fold the turned fabric neatly and fold in the corners. The final stage is to lace the opposite edges to each other using under-and-over stitch. (If you used pins you can now remove them prior to placing the work in a frame.)

OTHER FRAMING INFORMATION

For the Candlescreen and the Mirror, the frames have been used as supplied. The Calendar frame was chosen to reflect a room's decor. However, the Clock and Square Tray have been re-sprayed using Aerosol Paint and there is no reason why you cannot use spray paint and other forms of decoration to brighten up frames. You can also use paper, attached using PVA glue, to decorate an entire frame. Coloured textured paper is very good for this purpose. This suggestion is made here because all too often pieces of work are placed by professional framers in dark, drab

frames, so I hope you will seize the opportunity to do something a little different to enhance your work.

CUSHION-MAKING

(Picture and Cushion)

Carefully press the back of your work with a damp cloth and a warm iron. Trim the tapestry canvas to leave a ½ in (1 cm) border for the seam. Cut your backing fabric to the same size. Place the right sides together and use basting stitches to secure the two pieces. Machine stitch the top and two sides of the cushion. Remove the basting stitches from the bottom edge and turn the cushion right side out. Make the tassels (four small ones for the top edge and four larger ones for the bottom). Attach the tassels to the cushion. Press the seam allowance on the bottom edge, place the cushion pad inside the cushion and close up the bottom edge with small stitches of oversewing.

CAFETIÈRE COVER

Make a 'sandwich' of stitched work, wadding and backing fabric. Secure the outer edges with basting stitches. Attach the satin bias binding to the right side of your work to create an outer edge suitable for the size of your individual cafetière. Trim the 'sandwich' to ¼ in (0.5 cm) of your bias binding stitch line. Hem the bias binding with tiny slip stitches. Attach the Velcro strips to the inside of the cover. Place the cover around the cafetière and trim off any excess Velcro.

Acknowledgements

Writing a book, although a seemingly solitary exercise, is always a combined effort in a variety of ways. The inspiration for the book was BBC TV's *Animal Hospital* series in which Rolf Harris introduced viewers to the work of the RSPCA Hospital and Rescue Services. The Head of the Veterinary Staff at the Harold Harmsworth Memorial Hospital (where the programmes were filmed) is David Grant, who has kindly written a *Foreword* for the book, and I would like to thank him and all his staff for being the inspiration behind the project and for doing such valuable work.

For their more 'hands-on' involvement I would like to thank Fran Huxley who liaised on behalf of the RSPCA, David Roberts and Sally Potter of Michael O'Mara Books and, of course, Doreen Montgomery. For their wonderful practical assistance my thanks go to Cara Ackerman of DMC Creative World, Sarah Gray of Framecraft Miniatures, Lora Verner Designs, and John Jay and his staff. Rebecca, Tess, Sue and Jean have all made major contributions and the magazine, *All About Cats* has also played a part as have Tony and Margaret. Two final mentions and 'thank you's' go to Susan Shanks, for continuing to promote my work in magazines, and to Peter Rogers.

124

Suppliers

DMC PRODUCTS

DMC Creative World Ltd
62 Pullman Road,
Wigston,
Leicester LE8 2DY
England.
Tel 0116 281 1040
Fax 0116 281 3592

DMC
51-66 Carrington Road,
Marrickville,
New South Wales 2204,
Australia.
Tel 00 612 559 3088
Fax 00 612 559 5338

SATC
43 Somerset Road,
PO Box 3868,
Capetown 8000,
South Africa.
Tel 00 272 141 98040
Fax 00 272 141 98047

DMC
7-9 Rue du Pavillion,
B-1210 Brussels,
Belgium.
Tel 00 322 2169 145
Fax 00 332 2451 707

BTW
Stader Landstr 41-43,
D-2820
Bremen 77,
Germany.
Tel 00 494 2163 2056
Fax 00 494 2163 4408

DMC
Viale Italia 84,
I-20020 Lainate,
Milano,
Italy.
Tel 00 392 9357 0427/28/29
Fax 00 392 9357 0398

DMC
Travessa de Escola,
Aràujo 36-A,
P-1100 Lisbon,
Portugal.
Tel 00 351 1356 0311
Fax 00 351 1355 6788

DMC (Needlecraft Asia Pte. Ltd)
63 Hillview Ave 01-03,
Lam Soon Industrial Building,
Singapore 2366.
Tel 00 657 640855
Fax 00 657 648550

The DMC Corporation
Port Kearny,
Building 10,
South Kearny,
New Jersey 07032,
USA.
Tel 001 201 589 0606
Fax 001 201 589 8931

FOR FRAMECRAFT PRODUCTS

Framecraft Minatures Ltd
372-376 Summer Lane,
Hockley,
Birmingham B19 3QA,
England.
Tel 0121 212 0551
Fax 0121 212 0552

Anne Brinkley Designs Inc
12 Chestnut Hill Lane,
Lincroft,
NJ 07738,
USA.
Tel 001 908 530 5432
Fax 001 908 530 3899

Gay Bowles Sales Inc
P O Box 1060,
Janesville,
WI 53547,
USA.
Tel 001 608 754 9212
Fax 001 608 754 0665

Ireland Needlecraft Pty Ltd
4, 2-4 Keppel Drive,
Hallam,
Vic 3803,
Australia.
Tel 0061 3 702 3222
Fax 0061 3 702 3255

Roland de Liever
Rue St Georges 10,
5380 Hemptinne-Fernelmont,
Belgium.
Tel 0032 81 85 55 79
Fax 0032 81 85 55 79

Anne Staar Collection
8 Avenue Des Frenes,
B1950 Kraainem,
Belgium.
Tel 0032 2 782 12 81
Fax 0032 2 731 71 60

Duraplast Distributors Inc
PO Box 75279,
White Rock,
British Columbia V4A 9N4,
Canada.
Tel 001 604 536 2251
Fax 001 604 536 2251

Carl J Permin a/s
28 Egegardsvej,
DK 2610 Rodovre,
Denmark.
Tel 0045 36721200
Fax 0045 36720088

Eva Rosenstand a/s
Virumgardsvej 18,
2830 Virum,
Denmark.
Tel 0045 42852044
Fax 0045 42852249

DMC
10 Avenue Ledru Rollin,
75012 Paris,
France.
Tel 0033 1 49 28 10 00
Fax 0033 1 43 42 54 36

Framecraft Deutschland
Bayerischer Platz 7,
10779 Berlin,
Germany.
Tel 0049 30 8539869
Fax 0049 30 8531287

Engbert J Blok
Halsbeker Strasse 43,
26655 Westerstede BRD,
Germany.
Tel 0049 44 8873424
Fax 0049 44 8873425

Carl Permin BV
Spinveld 1 a,
4825 HR Breda,
Holland.
Tel 0031 76 221 820
Fax 0031 76 221 703

Lanarte
Einsteinweg 1,
8912 AP Leeuwarden,
Holland.
Tel 0031 58 936935
Fax 0031 58 151211

DMC
Viale Italia 84,
1-20020 Lainate,
Milano,
Italy.
Tel 0039 2 93570427
Fax 0039 2 93570398

Sanyei Imports
2-64 Hirakata,
Fukuju-Cho,
Hashima Shi,
Gifu,
Japan.
Tel 0081 583985144
Fax 0081 583985132

The Embroidery Shop
286 Queen Street,
Masterton,
New Zealand.
Tel 0064 6 377 1418
Fax 0064 6 377 1418

Bimbi Garcia Polo
C/Hermosilla 49,
28001 Madrid,
Spain.
Tel 0034 1 576 2769
Fax 0034 1 576 5036

DMC
Fontanolla 21-23,
08010 Barcelona,
Spain.
Tel 0034 93 317 7436
Fax 0034 93 302 5023

FOR GREETING CARDS
Lora Verner Designs
Worldheath Limited
18 South Hill Park,
Hampstead,
London NW3 2SB
England.
Tel 0171 794 3537
Fax 0171 794 8646

Conversion Table
For Six Strand Embroidery Thread

This conversion table should only be used as a guide as it is not always possible to provide exact comparisons. Nearest equivalent shades are marked*.

DMC	Anchor	DMC	Anchor	DMC	Anchor	DMC	Anchor	DMC	Anchor
BLANC	2	453	231	733	280*	892	28	3042	870
ECRU	387	470	267*	738	361	893	41	3045	888
B5200	1	471	266*	739	366	902	897*	3046	887
94	1216	472	253*	741	304	904	258	3053	858*
111	1243	501	878	742	303	905	257	3072	847*
113	1210	503	875*	743	302	906	256*	3346	267*
209	109	504	1042	744	301	920	1002	3347	266*
210	108	523	859*	745	300	921	884*	3348	264
304	1006	535	1041*	746	275	931	1034	3364	260*
310	403	543	933	758	9575*	934	862*	3371	382
315	1019*	550	101	760	1022	935	861	3609	85
318	399	552	99	761	1021	947	330	3712	1023
320	215	553	98	762	234	948	1011	3746	1030
333	119	606	335	772	259	950	4146	3768	779
334	977	608	332*	775	128	951	1010	3772	1007
335	38	611	898	791	178	957	50*	3776	1048
340	118	613	831	792	941	964	185	3778	1013
341	117	640	903*	793	176	972	298	3779	868
349	13*	642	392	798	131	973	297	3782	388
350	11*	644	830	799	136	976	1001	3787	393*
353	6	645	273	807	168*	977	1002	3790	393*
368	214	646	8581*	817	13*	987	244	3799	236
371	854	647	1040	822	390	988	243	3801	35*
407	914	648	900	825	162*	989	242	3802	1019*
414	235	666	46	831	277*	996	433	3803	972
422	943*	676	891	833	907*	3012	844	3815	877
434	310*	677	886	834	874	3013	842	3817	875*
435	1046	703	238	838	380	3021	905	3820	306
436	1045	712	926	839	360*	3023	899*	3821	305*
437	362	725	305	840	379	3024	397	3823	386
444	290	726	295*	841	378	3031	360*	3827	363
451	233	727	293	844	1041*	3033	391	3828	943*